Win-Win Games for All Ages

Cooperative Activities for Building Social Skills

Josette and Ba Luvmour

with

Debra & Tom Weistar

and Amber & Albee Kara

NEW SOCIETY PUBLISHERS

Cataloguing in Publication Data:
A catalog record for this publication is available from the National
Library of Canada.

Cover design by Diane McIntosh; cover image: Eyewire

Printed in Canada by Friesens Inc. Second Printing March, 2005.

New Society Publishers acknowledges the support of the Government of
Canada through the Book Publishing Industry Development Program
(BPIDP) for our publishing activities,
and the assistance of the Province of
British Columbia through the British
Columbia Arts Council.

**BRITISH
COLUMBIA
ARTS COUNCIL**
Supported by the Province of British Columbia

Paperback ISBN: 0-86571-441-x

Inquiries regarding requests to reprint all or part of *Win-Win Games*
should be addressed to New Society Publishers at the address below.

To order directly from the publishers, please call toll-free (North
America) 1-800-567-6772, or order online at www.newsociety.com

Any other inquiries can be directed by mail to:

New Society Publishers
P.O. Box 189, Gabriola Island, BC V0R 1X0, Canada

New Society Publishers' mission is to publish books that contribute
in fundamental ways to building an ecologically sustainable and
just society, and to do so with the least possible impact on the
environment, in a manner that models this vision. We are committed to
doing this not just through education, but through action. We are acting on our commitment to the world's remaining ancient forests
by phasing out our paper supply from ancient forests worldwide.
This book is one step towards ending global deforestation and climate
change. It is printed on acid-free paper that is **100% old growth
forest-free** (100% post-consumer recycled), processed chlorine
free, and printed with vegetable based, low VOC inks. For further information, or to browse our full list of books and purchase securely, visit
our website at: www.newsociety.com

NEW SOCIETY PUBLISHERS   www.newsociety.com

CONTENTS

INTRODUCTION

THE AIM OF *Win-Win Games for All Ages* is to offer cooperative games and activities that can deepen relationships. We have designed the activities primarily for groups of children, but many of them can be used for adults only. Naturally, they work very well with groups of mixed ages. All of the Cooperative Games and Activities, Initiatives, and Holistic Learning Adventures you will find here are set up to support well-being in each participant while honoring the developmental capacities of children.

The intention of our first book, *Everyone Wins*, was to enhance self-esteem, help resolve conflict, and aid in communication. *Win-Win Games for All Ages* aims to empower people to understand and appreciate one another — a persistent need in our increasingly depersonalized and simultaneously multiethnic world. This is a more profound and subtle goal, yet well within the reach of parents, teachers, and group leaders. We might even say that it must be reached to allow harmonious human relationships.

We are not born knowing how to get along and understand each other. Indeed, in North American culture, we learn early how to compete against each other. And as a society, we struggle with the friction caused by our wish for democracy and the actuality of extending its privileges to those people outside the dominant hierarchy. If we are to learn how to live together harmoniously, then we must change some of our old ways of doing things and learn new ways of relating to each other. And that requires a learning environment that supports transformation. Such an environment must simultaneously offer safety while it fosters trust, honest expression, and straightforwardness. People must have an opportunity to discover ways to hear values, demonstrate skills, and self-express in safety — important skills that can serve for a lifetime. Let us use a description of a Family Camp to illustrate how the resources in *Win-Win Games for All Ages* create the conditions necessary for transformation to occur.

Typically, we begin a Family Camp by gathering everyone in the meadow to play "Character Cards." We break into groups of approximately 12 players each; everyone plays (including the staff), and family members stay together. The cards for this game are a broad assortment of cartoon characters, super-heroes, and cultural icons that represent a spectrum of human personality traits. Players select three cards each. Taking turns, each person tells the reasons for his or her particular choices. Players of all ages catch on quickly and there is often great fun and banter. Not surprisingly, everyone learns a bit about each other. On another level, though, we are establishing the legitimacy of people talking about themselves without interruption or interpretation.

Next we choose games that, on the surface, appear goofy and insignificant. It might be "Bumpity-Bump" or a tag game or both. Yet, despite the frivolity, many important social interactions take place. People touch one another in safe ways. They get to appear ridiculous without shame, which for many is an entirely new experience. In this way, participants get a sense of the equality that will be present throughout camp — an equality brought about because these games, as with all the Cooperative Games and Activities, call upon skills that people of all ages possess.

On the second day of Family Camp, we move into Initiatives, a higher risk activity. An Initiative is essentially a problem-solving activity that requires a statement of values by each player, the creation of a strategy, and a skillful execution of that strategy. Family members work together in groups of approximately 12 players; this time, staff members do not play.

Initiatives produce a microcosm of the dynamics of any group and can be used to foster trust and create a "safe space" for risk taking. "Dream Bucket," for instance, has participants collect an object from nature that represents a dream or hope they have for their family. Each participant names what the object represents before placing it in a bucket. The filled bucket goes in the middle of a 16-foot (5-meter) diameter circle, and participants must use an assortment of tools — ropes, pieces of inner tube, etc. — to rescue their dreams without crossing the boundary of the circle. We remind everyone that they are playing a game and that the most important part of the game is the relationship among the players. Though there are many possible solutions to "Dream Bucket," all require participation from the small and young, as well as from the strong and old.

The dynamics in the game mirror the real-life dynamics of the participating families and of the group as a whole. Not everyone has fun all the time, just as people will often have difficulty with the way decisions are made in life. But the fact that most participants find a way to express their difficulty indicates that a measure of safety has been established — an underlying reason for presenting the Initiative in the first place. And when they rescue the bucket, participants often express feelings of accomplishment and fun.

The activities we choose to use in Family Camp fulfill very specific purposes in creating a useful learning environment. Each type of engagement requires increasing risk taking. As facilitators and leaders, then, we assess groups carefully and choose appropriate activities. We are equally careful in our "framing" and "debriefing" — the ways in which we introduce and then later discuss the activities.

Framing

The Cooperative Games and Activities are used for everything from simple play or the deepening of friendships to diagnosing a group's social climate, so we always consider framing when using them. Framing helps to set the intention for a game or activity and allows a group to set goals.

Game Leaders are responsible for framing a game or activity for the group. For example, depending on circumstances, a Game Leader might frame "Love Your Neighbor" as a warm-up exercise, with no particular focus beyond that of having fun, or as an exercise so that participants can build trust and get to know each other better. In either case, the Game Leader has created a frame in which to observe and later to debrief the group.

Debriefing

Risk taking is always the most important factor in learning to open oneself to others, and in learning to appreciate others. Debriefing creates a forum that allows people to talk about and understand the risks they and others have taken during the activities. It also increases safety and straightforwardness by encouraging discussion at the end of each activity for reviewing what did and did not work for each participant. And it allows adjustments to the next activity that will increase everyone's success. When we debrief "Dream Bucket," for instance (which we always do), some common themes emerge, including communication patterns, fairness, and the qualities that make an activity enjoyable. Frequently, family members are able to name deeper family patterns, but trust is not usually well enough established to allow a full exploration of the dynamics.

It is the facilitator's job to protect everyone's right to speak and to make sure that the relevant people acknowledge what is said. Debriefing consists primarily of asking questions, paraphrasing, and sensitively inviting all participants with pertinent perspectives to contribute. Debriefing attends to each person and to the issues at hand; thus, there should be no outside interruptions. When emotions are strong, it is usually best to go slowly and let them be felt by the group. If someone has difficulty articulating a feeling, it is good to quietly offer words that might enrich the meaning or to ask questions to help the individual find the appropriate words.

In general, we caution against solution seeking while in the process of debriefing. The temptation to resolve conflict too quickly can be particularly strong for a facilitator: one feels the anguish of the participants, especially the children, and hopes to offer them a better way by imparting a communication technique or by pointing out healthier ethical and moral responses. In our experience, though, most attempts to resolve conflict in these ways end up disempowering the very people they are meant to help.

We have begun to understand why premature solution seeking has such a negative effect. The purpose of any Initiative is to develop meaningful relationships which, to us, means developing intrinsic capacities and talents. An imposed "teaching" does not allow the development of a person's inherent powers of discrimination and responsiveness and does not nurture self-knowledge. Rather, it has a hidden subtext of lack of trust. To bribe or coerce children (or anyone) into accepting a teaching because an extrinsic source insists upon it says that the individual is incapable of coming to understanding on his or her own. Furthermore, extrinsic teaching reinforces hierarchical power structures. Instead of a community of learners, we end up with privileged "teachers" and underprivileged "students." Condescension and lack of trust (no matter how well intentioned) poison learning — especially emotional learning.

Also, solution seeking sends the message that intensity of feeling is somehow bad. Most people wrongly assume that emotional intensity signals discomfort and is a desperate request for a solution. It has been our repeated experience that only rarely does the person feeling the intensity desire a solution. More often, the intensity reflects a long-suffered wounding that is begging for expression, or it points to other problems not associated with that particular moment. In other words, there has been a build-up of negativity from one problem (or from a series of unrelated problems) that has found no outlet. The person then uses this moment, because there is finally some attention, to release pent-up energy. The point is that to attempt to resolve the matter often blocks full expression and thus leaves the person with a quick fix. And, as quick fixes notoriously lead to more difficulties, one could argue that the resolution has worsened the situation.

While we candidly admit that activities sometimes raise issues that are beyond the skill level of the facilitator to process, most issues can and must be handled within the group. Indeed, most learning happens during debriefing, when we sit down and talk about our time together. In our experience, the group often has insights beyond those that any individual, facilitator, or clique could offer — a realization that can become a new source of empowerment for everyone. Perhaps for these reasons, after debriefing, perspectives will often shift toward self-knowledge and participants will report deeper communication among family members. Of course, there may be rare instances when an issue does arise that is beyond the capacity of any person to deal with in a healthy way. In those cases, we suggest that you seek outside help for safety and completion.

Our experience has taught us that resolutions arise best in a community of learners when each person contributes according to his or her intrinsic capacity and talent. For example, we have all likely heard a child tell his or her parents that they are being unfair. Unfortunately, such words are usually spoken in anger or defeat. The accusation may lead to a temporary solution, with the parents promising to try

harder or with the child promising to word his request so
that the parents can "hear it." But in debriefing, something
else often happens. The child can often describe, in detail,
the dynamics of the entire situation and, if met with patience
and the genuine interest of others, can speak of his or her
feelings as each aspect of an event unfolded.

Consider, for instance, the experience of a young girl who
played "Dream Bucket" with her family. She saw her sibling
pout and watched her mother worry about it. She felt appre-
hensive, since a typical family dynamic was about to play
out. She tried harder to hold her father's attention, out of
fear that he would turn to her mother and sister. When he
did, she complained. She watched her father's frustration
grow until, as he often did, he acted by making arbitrary
decisions — in this case, about how to rescue the Dream
Bucket.

Look how brilliant the young girl is. No one taught her
in a lesson plan how to read emotional content and context
so clearly. No one taught her the intelligent interventions she
attempted as she tried to prevent unfairness from occurring.
These sprang forth from her innate talents and capacities.

Consider another example that comes from our ongoing
work with those older teens who are in low security lock-up
for having committed felonies. When these teens arrive at
camp, they often arrive in the company of their warden.
Intense hierarchies, based on physical prowess, dominate the
group. As always, we do not use any form of reward or pun-
ishment. When difficulties arise, everyone must work
through them in the moment, learning as we go and from our
experience.

Sometimes, we will ask the most physically intimidating
teen to play a game such as "Two Truths and a Lie," which
requires emotional involvement. Or an Initiative will call for
physical skills other than sheer strength. Embarrassment is
obvious and often transforming when that teen sees someone

of lower status engage the task. Indeed, it is a compelling moment for everyone, and debriefing the event is invariably interesting.

As did the young girl in our first example, the teens usually understand the dynamics of everyone very well. The anticipation, feelings, and reactions are seen by many, not just the principals. Often, someone will have the courage to bring up the way status is accorded in the group; if not, we do. Typically, no one will admit to any dramatic change, but it is nevertheless obvious that change has occurred — in attitudes and elsewhere. People who before were ordered about are now spoken to respectfully. Swaggering and bullying diminish; mistakes are more easily tolerated. And (a bonus for us), it becomes less difficult to get participants to debrief further activities.

To those involved in Holistic Education, the young girl's experience and that of the teens are examples of experiential education. Many people think that experiential education means one learns through sensory motor skills and project creation: build a canoe, for instance, and learn about math, carpentry, water dynamics, etc. But there is more to experiential education: it must include an increase in self-knowledge.

Who we are as we do is more important than the doing, no matter how creative the doing. The activities that we engage in at Family Camp call forth our intrinsic qualities, and debriefing allows us to name these capacities as part of our lives. Debriefing, then, is integral to a learning environment that supports transformation. The safety, trust, and openness established during the activities serve as a platform to afford participants a deepening appreciation of relationship and set the stage for the possibility of transformation. And deepening relationship and transformation are what *Win-Win Games for All Ages* is about.

EnCompass — Our View of Relationship

At EnCompass, we embrace holism and hold Ultimacy as the aim of all learning. Holism holds that the whole is more than the sum of its parts and that the synergy of all aspects of being leads to profound self-knowledge. Abraham Maslow called this synergy "self-actualization"; Carl Rogers referred to it as a "fully functioning person." At EnCompass we use the term "Ultimacy." Originally coined by Paul Tillich in 1957 (but brought into our world by our colleague Scott Forbes), "Ultimacy" refers to the actualization that can occur when the whole of who we are is nurtured and we experience well-being. Consequently, in all our work, we support the well-being of the physical, emotional, psychological, intellectual, social, and spiritual aspects of a person, while realizing that the synergy of these aspects is unique and mysterious.

In order to meet the demands of Holistic Education, EnCompass has programs that reach into all learning environments. Our work in holistic child development — Natural Learning Rhythms — informs our programs, which include outdoor education, three levels of Natural Learning Rhythms Seminars, Rites of Passage for both adults and teens, Family Camp, Family Weekend, counseling and therapy, several teen challenge and leadership courses, and Inspirational Journeys for preteens. Our new Education Center has just opened and houses a school for children from 6 to 13 years of age, a research team that is investigating Holistic Education, and a Teacher Development program to help teachers in traditional venues bring holistic practices into their classrooms.

Relationship defines our organization. We hold relationships as sacred: they provide the moment where theory meets practice meets actuality. Our programs bring us into contact with many people, and we have to be sensitive and precise about the modes of contact we choose to use. If the relationships among all the people associated with EnCompass —

staff, clients, friends, and donors — were not cared for, then we would not be creating the opportunity to actualize Ultimacy and would be failing in our intent. Thus when we say that we have high regard for the Cooperative Games and Activities, Initiatives, and Holistic Learning Adventures described in this book, we mean that used with care and intelligence, they can serve well-being and help facilitate holistic, human-to-human connection.

Layout of the Book

The activities in *Win-Win Games for All Ages* are divided into three sections, each with its own introduction and unique format. The sections are: Cooperative Games and Activities; Initiatives; and Holistic Learning Adventures.

Various degrees of interpersonal risk taking are required for any of the activities in the book. For clarity and to facilitate the selection process, activities in each section appear in ascending order from least risky to most risky.

Information that will help you to evaluate an activity's usefulness in different situations follows the title of each Game or Initiative. The information is organized into the following categories (all categories do not necessarily appear for each activity).

Age level refers to the minimum age a participant needs to be to enjoy the game. All age levels are just a guideline: you know your players and can choose games accordingly.

Group Size refers to the minimum number of players necessary to play the game.

Activity Level rates the amount of effort required for the game, on a scale from one to five. The "1s" are tag games that require a lot of running and energy; the "5s" are sitting games that require very little activity.

Location refers to where the game is best played: inside and/or outside.

Supplies refer to what you will need in order to play the game or accomplish the task.

Set-Up indicates how supplies and other props must be set up in order for the game to be played.

Description tells you how to play a game or complete an initiative.

Variation describes other versions of the game or initiative. Any variations used with an initiative ought to be carefully considered before using.

Framing and Debriefing provides information that can help increase the effectiveness of an initiative. Initiatives often reveal interpersonal dynamics within a group which, if processed with care, can foster closer relationships and trust.

Note contains additional information of a useful nature.

We also describe three Holistic Learning Adventures (all of which have been used at EnCompass): "What Is a Tree?"; "What Is a Culture?"; and "Wilderness and Wildness." Each description contains a brief comment on Holistic Education as an educational priority in the development of a person and his or her interpersonal skills. The Holistic Learning Adventures are described in prose, with an emphasis on embedded activities and debriefing opportunities.

COOPERATIVE GAMES AND ACTIVITIES

READERS OF OUR FIRST BOOK, *Everyone Wins*, know that we greatly appreciate cooperative games and activities for their ability to enhance communication, develop academic skills, and resolve conflict. They allow safe ways for people to talk with one another about difficult issues. They are fun. They include everyone, and differing skills enhance their value. Participants come to understand that everyone has something to contribute and that each contribution makes the game more enjoyable for all.

The following cooperative games and activities have been carefully selected to foster the deepening of interpersonal relationships. This can be best achieved by deliberately creating a sequence of games that proceed from the less risky to the more risky. It often works best to play one or two very active low-risk games first, in order to build trust among players. Do not be misled or lulled, though: significant interpersonal learning can occur during even the least risky of games.

Framing determines much of the value of a game. By using story or by simply mentioning that a particular facet of a game is important, a facilitator can remind players about central aspects of relationship. Those aspects include the feelings that arise while playing; body language; and the touch, tone, and intent implicit in any communication. If players know they will be expected to reflect on the game (debrief), then they will often pay more attention to the interactions

13

that occur among other members of the group. We suggest that you simply use trial and error, and soon you will be a skillful framer.

Finally, there is the matter of safety. We have not included comments about physical safety, except in some of the notes where we believe the necessary precautions may not be obvious. Do remember to inspect your playing fields for hazards. Make sure that participants do not have any injury or disability that might lead to problems or prevent them from playing. Remind bigger participants to watch out for smaller participants, especially in highly active games.

Dead Man's Ball

Age Level: 7+

Group Size: 10+

Activity Level: 1

Location: Outside

Supplies: Soft objects to use as projectiles. Nerf balls and other small foam objects work best. This game requires at least two objects and can include as many as the group can handle. A rough guide would be one object for every six people.

Set-Up: A large field with clearly defined boundaries.

Description: For the sake of description, we will assume a group of 15 players and three Nerf balls. The game begins with any three people holding the balls. The object of the game is to get as many people "Down" as possible. To get a person "Down," one of the players must throw a ball and hit another player with it. When a player is hit, they must go "Down" on one knee. The only way that player can get up is if the player who got him or her "Down" goes "Down" themselves. Let us say that Player One hits Players Two, Three, and Four. They are "Down." But then Player Five throws a ball and hits Player One. Players Two, Three, and Four are then "Up" and can play once more.

A downed player can pick up a ball as it rolls past, but cannot move from their spot. If a downed player has a ball, he or she can try and convince one of the "Up" players to get the player who got them. The game goes on until everyone is tired or there is one person left with all the balls and everyone else is "Down." Then the game restarts.

If a player catches a thrown ball, then the player who threw the ball must go "Down." A player with a ball can deflect other balls thrown at them with the ball they have, and then neither player goes "Down." If a ball bounces off the ground and hits a player, then it does not count. If a ball is thrown and misses its target, then it is fair game: anyone can grab it.

Note: *This game is fun and energetic and needs at least one player who can keep the cooperative energy alive. The Game Leader should keep an eye out for overly rough or competitive players. It is a good idea to have a no-hit area on the body: no hits above the shoulders or in the groin area.*

Elbow Tag

Age Level: 4+

Group Size: 10-20

Activity Level: 1

Location: Outside

Supplies: None

Set-Up: Players pair up, hooking elbows. The whole group forms a big circle, allowing several feet of space between joined pairs. Pairs are stationary.

Description: The game begins with a Tagger and a Runner. The Runner becomes "Safe" when hooking elbows with one of the paired players. When the Runner hooks up to a pair, the player opposite is released and becomes the one being pursued by the Tagger. If the Tagger tags the Runner, they immediately switch roles.

Variation: Recommended for ages 9+, "Advanced Elbow Tag" is slightly more complicated but allows for a faster-paced game. In this version, when the Runner hooks up with a pair, the player opposite becomes the Tagger. In this way, the role of Tagger is constantly changing. Players must stay alert and react quickly to avoid getting tagged and becoming the Tagger.

Note: *Encourage quick hook-ups so that the game stays lively and everyone gets a chance to run. Players are sometimes shy about joining elbows; don't force them. Usually by the time the game gets going everyone is hooking up to each other, and self-consciousness diminishes. "Elbow Tag" allows for safe touching, and through the excitement of the game, players hook up with others that they would not ordinarily choose to be close to, helping to break down artificial barriers to connection.*

Clam-Free Tag

Age Level: 3+

Group Size: 10-40

Activity Level: 1

Location: Outside

Supplies: Tagger objects

Set-Up: Give tagger objects to approximately one-sixth of the group.

Description: The Taggers chase the whole group. Tagged players are "Frozen" and remain "Frozen" until two other players release them by joining hands to form a circle over the tagged players' heads and lowering their hands to the ground. The "Frozen" player steps out of their circle and resumes play. Players cannot be tagged while unfreezing another player. A player who has been tagged and released three times becomes the Tagger when tagged a fourth time.

Note: *This game is especially well suited for mixed ages such as family groups. Great for the little ones but fun for all. Encourages spontaneous helping and watching out for others. Take note of players who help others and players who run away without stopping to help.*

Help-Me Tag

Age Level: 4+

Group Size: 10-30

Activity Level: 1

Location: Outside

Supplies: Enough soft balls (or other suitable objects) to have one ball for every three players, plus different objects to identify the Taggers.

Set-Up: Start in a circle. Pass the balls or objects to about one-third of the group. Pass the tagger objects to approximately one-sixth of the group. (One Tagger for every six to eight players.)

Description: The object of this tag game is to help others, hence the name "Help-Me Tag." The Taggers chase the whole group. A player is "Safe" if holding one of the balls (only one player per ball); anyone not holding a ball is open for tagging. A player who is tagged takes the tagging object, turns three times slowly, and loudly calls out, "I've been tagged" (this gives the first Tagger time to get away). The tagged player can then pursue others.

Note: *Watch for risk taking and players' willingness to help others. Will players risk getting tagged to help another player? Are there some players that hold a ball the whole game to avoid getting tagged? "Help-Me Tag" is a good lead-in game for "Hug Tag" (see* Everyone Wins*) and is a great game for opening a discussion on helping one another and how that may lead to trust and friendship.*

Amoeba Tag

Age Level: 5+

Group Size: 10-50

Activity Level: 1

Location: Outside

Supplies: None

Set-Up: None

Description: The game begins with one Tagger. When the Tagger tags a player, they join hands and continue to run after and tag other players. Play continues until the "amoeba" grows to four players. The players then break into two pairs. Each pair continues tagging until it becomes four players, and then they split into two pairs again, and so on until there is only one player left to tag. That player starts the game again, becoming the first part of the amoeba .

Variation: The amoeba can get bigger and bigger and never split into smaller units. Before you try this variation, commonly called "Blob Tag," make sure that the group is ready for a high level of cooperation and is watching out for each other.

Note: *This game requires a fairly high degree of cooperation and taking care with one another, especially when two or three players are joined as a tagging amoeba. What is the priority for the group? Do they try to tag another player regardless of what their partner(s) are capable of?*

Tube Tag

Age Level: 10+

Group Size: 10-20

Activity Level: 1

Location: Outside

Supplies: Bicycle tire tubes (valve removed); half as many as the size of the group. One tagger object for every six players or for every three pairs.

Set-Up: The group forms into pairs. Each pair is given a tube. After explaining the game, give the pairs time to practice with each other.

Description: Pairs get inside the tire tubes. Pairs form a circle, with the Tagger pairs in the center to start. The game begins when a Tagger pair tries to tag another pair. When tagged, the tagged pair becomes the new Tagger pair. The new pair holds up a tagging object and declares, "We've been tagged!" (three times) to allow the other pair to get away.

Note: *This is a walking tag game. Monitor closely. A high degree of cooperation is necessary. Remind the group not to run but to power walk (fast, powerful walking strides). Let participants talk about what they learned about teamwork or their partners.*

Team Tag

Age Level: 14+

Group Size: 15-21

Activity Level: 1

Location: Outside

Supplies: None

Set-Up: Divide the group into groups of three players; these are teams. If the group isn't divisible by three, then have one team of two players that are physically strong or adept. (It is the Game Leader's responsibility to create or rearrange teams so that they are relatively equal in ability.) After explaining the game, give the teams two to three minutes to strategize and come up with ideas for teamwork. After each round, give them time to re-strategize.

Description: In this tag game, everyone is a Tagger. Players can tag anyone except those on their team. When a player is tagged, that player must go "Down" on one knee in the place they were tagged, "Frozen." The only way they can become unfrozen is to receive a High-Ten from one of their team members. In the case of simultaneous tags, if there is a dispute as to who tagged whom, then both players go "Down." A player may not fake being tagged and "Frozen."

When all three members of a team are tagged and "Down," they are "Out" for that round. The round continues until only one team remains. When the field is reduced to two or three teams, have the rest of the group create a smaller tagging area by encircling the other teams.

Note: *This game can be highly competitive, although, as with team sports, there is also a high degree of cooperation possible within any given team. Best for mature groups that can handle the competition aspect well. "Team Tag" can stimulate valuable discussion about sides, equality, competition, war, and peace.*

Hoochie-Coochie

Age Level: 8+

Group Size: 7-12

Activity Level: 3

Location: Inside or outside

Supplies: Objects to sit on. Some examples are carpet squares, wooden disks, or pillows. Chairs work, too.

Set-Up: Players sit in a circle.

Description: Each seat in the circle has a motion and a sound associated with it. Before the game starts, the person occupying each seat establishes the motion and sound that will belong to that space throughout the game, except for the person in the Hoochie-Coochie seat. That seat has the following preset motion and sound associated with it: a tickling motion made with the index and middle fingers under the chin of the person to the left of the seat, along with the phrase, "Hoochie-Coochie." Starting to the right of the "Hoochie-Coochie Master" (HCM) each person invents a sound/motion combination until the circle is complete.

The facilitator acts as the HCM to begin the game. The HCM performs the Hoochie-Coochie motion and sound, and then performs the motion and sound associated with any other place in the circle. The person sitting in the space associated with the HCM's second motion and sound repeats the action associated with their seat (in a reasonably short amount of time, usually less than five seconds) and then performs the motion/sound for any other seat in the circle (including the Hoochie-Coochie seat). Play proceeds until someone messes up.

If someone performs his or her own or another's motion/sound incorrectly, play stops, and that person moves to the seat just to the right of the HCM. The people between the empty seat and the HCM must move one seat to the right.

The HCM is the judge of when another player messes up. If a player makes a mistake and the HCM doesn't notice, then other players must keep quiet. If the HCM messes up and others notice, then anyone can stop play and unseat the HCM. In that case, the person in the HCM seat (and everyone else) moves one seat to the right, thus giving the game a new HCM. Play can continue indefinitely.

Note: *Extra players can be rotated into the seat to the right of the HCM: If someone in the circle messes up, then they go "Out" and the first person waiting in the queue moves into the game. The player who is "Out" then moves to the end of the queue to await another chance.*

This Is My Nose

Age Level: 6+

Group Size: 8-20

Activity Level: 3

Location: Inside or outside

Supplies: None

Set-Up: The group forms a circle, standing shoulder to shoulder. The Game Leader starts in the center of the circle.

Description: The object of "This Is My Nose" is to avoid becoming the player in the middle. To begin the game, the Game Leader walks up to a player in the circle, points to his or her own elbow and says, "This is my nose." The player must point to his or her nose and say, "This is my elbow." The Game Leader then goes up to a different player, points to another body part, and misnames it (points to his or her finger, for instance, and says, "This is my shoulder.") The player must respond correctly or become the new player in the middle. In order to move out of the middle, the new player in the middle must make a player in the circle mess up and say or point to the wrong body part. When this happens, the player takes the place of the person who made the error.

Note: *The game can be used as an anatomy lesson. Depending on the age of the players, body part names can be more scientific: "patella" instead of "knee"; "epidermis" instead of "skin"; "clavicle" instead of "collarbone."*

Bumpity-Bump

Age Level: 10+

Group Size: 10-30

Activity Level: 2

Location: Inside or outside

Supplies: None

Set-Up: The group forms a circle, standing shoulder to shoulder. Player One starts in the center.

Description: Player One walks up to a player on the circle (Player Two) and says one of four things: "Left," "Right," "Straight," or "Center," followed immediately by the phrase, "Bumpity-Bump, Bump, Bump." Player Two must make the correct response before Player One finishes saying "Bumpity-Bump, Bump, Bump." The correct response for the command "Left" is the name of the player on Player Two's left; for "Right," it's the name of the player on his or her right; for "Straight," it's his or her own name; and for "Center," it's the name of Player One (the player in the center). If Player Two responds correctly and in time, Player One goes on and repeats the process with another player. If Player Two responds incorrectly or too late, the two players switch places, and Player Two moves to the center and begins the process with another player.

Note: *For groups with 12 or more participants, have more than one player in the center at one time to keep the game interesting and engaging for all. This silly but challenging game is excellent for loosening up a group that is shy or not yet talking freely.*

Silent Name Game

Age Level: 12+

Group Size: 8+

Activity Level: 4

Location: Inside or outside

Supplies: None

Set-Up: Players pair up, preferably with someone they don't know well. Allow adequate space between pairs so that they do not disturb other pairs.

Description: Every player gets five minutes to learn as much as they can about their partner, while maintaining complete silence. Gestures and pantomime, writing in the dirt, and other creative forms of communication are allowed but no talking and no vocal sounds. When time is up, the group forms a circle. Partners introduce each other to the rest of the group and briefly relate some of what they have learned. Partners then have the chance to approve or correct the information given.

Note: *"Silent Name Game" is valuable for allowing the group to interact without the inhibitions that talking together can bring. This is a good activity to start with and for building relationship.*

Favorite F.I.V.E.S.

Age Level: 6+

Group Size: 10-20

Activity Level: 4

Location: Inside or outside

Supplies: None

Set-Up: Players pair up and sit together, preferably with someone they don't know well. Allow a little space between pairs.

Description: "Favorite F.I.V.E.S." is an acronym: "F" stands for film, "I" for interest, "V" for vocation, "E" for eats, and "S" for sport or song. One partner of each pair begins by asking the other what his or her "Favorite F.I.V.E.S." are: Favorite film, interests, vocation (what they would like to do for a living), eats (favorite food), and sport or song. Then they switch. Give pairs about six to eight minutes together. When everyone is done, re-group and form a circle. One by one, players introduce each other to the group, saying their partner's name, and their "Favorite F.I.V.E.S." The Game Leader gives each player the chance to correct any incorrect information.

Variation: Instead of relating their partner's "Favorite F.I.V.E.S." directly, ask players to tell the group what they have most in common and least in common with their partners. Or adapt one or more of the categories to better fit the group. For example, change "vocation" to "vacation" (What was your favorite family vacation?).

Note: *In this game, players are paired but are given specific instructions of what to talk about. This allows the pairs to talk freely with one another without having to think of what to say, thus increasing ease and enjoyment. This game often stimulates conversation that moves beyond the Favorite F.I.V.E.S.*

Nickname Game

Age Level: 10+

Group Size: 6-12

Activity Level: 4

Location: Inside or outside

Supplies: None

Set-Up: Have the group form a circle when ready for a quiet activity.

Description: The "Nickname Game" moves from player to player around the circle. Players say their name, then tell the rest of the group about a nickname they have or have had in the past, how they got it, and whether or not they like it.

Note: *The Game Leader should be the first to speak and should frame the activity carefully by telling the group that nicknames can be hurtful as well as endearing. Remind participants not to use players' nicknames unless they have permission to do so. This game offers an excellent opportunity for risk in telling the group where one is vulnerable in regard to name calling and respect of one's name, as well as opportunities for humor and a little self-directed fun making.*

Whom Do You Admire?

Age Level: 14+

Group Size: 8-12

Activity Level: 4

Location: Inside or outside

Supplies: None

Set-Up: The group stands or sits in a circle. The Game Leader asks players to think of someone they admire. It is best if they think of someone whom others will recognize — someone out in the world at large. It can be a political figure, celebrity, entertainer, humanitarian, activist, author, etc., either living or dead.

Description: The Game Leader begins the game, saying his or her own name and the name of the person he or she admires. Play proceeds around the circle. Player One says the Game Leader's name and whom the Game Leader admires. Then Player One says his or her own name and the name of the person he or she admires. Player Two repeats what the Game Leader and Player One have said, then says his or her own name and the name of the person he or she admires. Play continues until everyone has had a turn. Then the Game Leader has to say everyone's name and whom they admire, in sequence.

Note: *The choice of whom to admire is, of course, up to each player. Some players choose family members, though it is better to encourage the choosing of well-known figures. This gives the rest of the group a better understanding of the player, which is one of the objectives of the game. Not everyone will recognize all figures.*

During the game, do not allow discussion or judgment of play-
ers' choices. After the game, in order to facilitate understanding
and knowledge of one another, discuss who the admired people
were and why they were chosen. To adapt the game for any age
group, simply change the topic. For example, when playing with
younger children, have them say their names and favorite ani-
mal or food.

Ally/Nemesis

Age Level: 10+

Group Size: 10-25

Activity Level: 3

Location: Inside or
outside

Supplies: None

Set-Up: None

Description: Have
the group form a
circle. Explain that

"Ally/Nemesis" is played in silence and that the silence begins
immediately. Ask participants to look around the group
slowly, looking at everyone. Then ask them to pick out one
person in the group, without indicating in any way whom
they have chosen. (If necessary, remind them to maintain
silence.)

After everyone has a person in mind, tell them that the
person they have chosen is their ally or friend. Repeat the
process, asking participants to choose a second, different person (still in silence). When everybody is ready, say that the
second person they have chosen is their nemesis. (You may

have to define "nemesis.") On the Game Leader's signal, the game begins.

The rules are simple: Everyone must keep their ally between them and their nemesis at all times. Everyone must remain silent, and not say whom their ally or nemesis is. Participants may move about as much as they like within the boundaries, as long as their ally is always between them and their nemesis. Begin each round with silence, choosing a new ally and nemesis.

Note: *This game is very subtle, and it is best played when a group is ready for a more thoughtful, though still active, game. Let it play out for a while, as it can shift as it is played — sometimes coming to a natural conclusion, often starting up again after a lull. Best played two or three times to allow the group to get the subtle aspects. Give participants time at the end to talk about the experience and to guess who chose them as their ally and nemesis. "Ally/Nemesis" is an excellent game for leading into discussions of friends and enemies, cliques, and how one knows when someone is their friend or not.*

Psychiatrist

Age Level: 13+

Group Size: 15-20

Activity Level: 4

Location: Inside or outside

Supplies: None

Set-Up: The group sits comfortably in a circle. The person chosen to be the Player leaves the group so that he or she cannot see or hear any explanation of the game.

Description: While the Player is away, the Game Leader explains the game to the rest of the group. When the Player returns, he or she is instructed to ask questions of individuals in the group. They must be "Yes" or "No" questions and they must be about the person (for example: "Do you have a sister?" or, "Are you wearing a green shirt?").

Players in the circle must answer as truthfully as they can, *but* they must answer as if they were the player to their left. For example, if the question is, "Do you have a sister?" and the player to your left does have a sister, the answer must be "Yes," even if you do not have a sister. If the player gives an incorrect answer, then the player on his or her left shouts "Psychiatrist!" and everyone jumps up and switches places.

The object of the game is for the Player to figure out that each group member is answering for the person on his or her left and that when "Psychiatrist!" is shouted and everyone moves, it is because of a wrong answer.

Note: *Group members should be fairly familiar with each other before playing this game, as it is sophisticated and subtle. Choose the Player carefully, since it will only work with someone who has never played the game before. Choose someone unlikely to catch on right away. Make sure that the Player asks everyone in the group a question at some point and that he or she doesn't just concentrate on a few players. Instruct participants to be subtle and not to look at the person to their left to check clothing, etc.; tell them to bluff if they do not know the correct answer. The Game Leader may need to suggest questions for the Player to ask.*

This game is engaging and focuses the group on one another in a total and encompassing way.

Camouflage

Age Level: 10+

Group Size: 10-20

Activity Level: 2

Location: Outside

Supplies: None

Set-Up: This game is played outdoors, preferably in a wooded area or one with heavy foliage.

Description: Choose one Player to start. The boundary for the Player is a three-foot (one-meter) diameter circle around where he or she is standing. The Player starts the game in a central area, eyes closed and ears covered, and counts loudly to 50. The rest of the group scatters throughout the wider area, looking for a place to hide. The only rule regarding hiding places is that participants must be in a position to see the Player at all times.

When the Player has finished counting, he or she starts to look for the camouflaged players but always from within the boundary circle. When the Player locates someone hidden, he or she points clearly and identifies the player by name (if known); if not, a description will suffice to alert the hidden player that he or she has been caught. Caught players wait in the central area until all are found. Another round begins with a new Player.

Note: *Frame this activity with a discussion about camouflage and the ways in which nature uses it to protect many creatures. Once the game is over, discuss what worked as true camouflage, the role that stillness played in hiding someone, and what the Player needed to do to find the others. To help deepen participants' understanding of one another, talk about the subtle aspects of nonverbal communication in getting to know a person better, or the ways in which we camouflage our feelings to hide from others.*

Love Your Neighbor

Age Level: 5+

Group Size: 8-15

Activity Level: 3

Location: Inside or outside

Supplies: None

Set-Up: Players form a circle standing up, shoulders almost touching. The Game Leader stands in the middle to explain and start the game.

Description: The player in the center (Player One) tries to get a place in the circle by following the rules of the game. If he or she is successful, then another player will end up in the center, and so on.

To begin play, Player One walks up to any player in the circle (Player Two) and asks, "Do you love your neighbor?" Player Two can respond with "Yes" or "No." A "Yes" response requires the players on either side of Player Two to switch places as quickly as they can, while Player One also tries to get into either space. Whoever is left without a space goes in the center and continues play.

If Player Two responds with "No," then Player One asks, "Then whom *do* you love?" Player Two responds with a statement that he or she makes up. For example, "I love everyone who has blue eyes," or "I love everyone who has ever cheated on a test." Anyone who can answer "Yes" to the statement (everyone with blue eyes, for example) has to find a new space in the circle. Whoever is left without a space moves to the center and gets to ask someone new, "Do you love your neighbor?"

Note: *Statements for "No" responses can refer to feelings or to personal experiences. When very young children are playing, physical aspects can also be used (such as eye color and clothing), but with older players, statements that can accelerate learning about each other are preferred. "Love Your Neighbor" allows a safe way for participants to reveal aspects of the self without undue attention and thus furthers group cohesion and understanding.*

Character Cards

Age Level: 6+

Group Size: 8-12

Activity Level: 4

Location: Inside or outside

Supplies: A packet of picture cards with a variety of different characters on them (cartoon characters, Star Wars, Disney, Super-heroes, etc.). You will need approximately 30 cards for a ten-person group, more if your group is larger.

Set-Up: Players sit in a circle. The Game Leader spreads the cards out, face up in the center of the circle, while explaining the game.

Description: Each player chooses one to three cards. The Game Leader tells players to choose characters that represent a part of themselves — their personality or character. When everyone has their card(s), players introduce themselves in turn to the rest of the group. They say their real name first, show the cards they have chosen, and explain how they are like the characters on the cards.

Note: *The Game Leader begins in order to set the tone, establish safety, model risk, and encourage meaningful explanations. "Character Cards" allows players to reveal their self-perceptions and identities; insecurities or labels are often stated through the character. If players are willing to risk, the game can deepen their understanding of one another. This game can be adapted for most ages.*

Signatures

Age Level: 11+

Group Size: 25-60

Activity Level: 3

Location: Inside or outside

Supplies: A list of approximately 25 tasks, with a space opposite each task for a signature; one list and a pencil for each player

Set-Up: Give each player a list and a pencil.

Description: The object is for players to get as many different signatures as possible (no duplicates) by completing tasks on the list. For example, one task might be to give someone in the group a High-Five. Once the task is complete, the player gets the signature of the player he High-Fived. Other examples of tasks: Get the signature of someone whose parents have the same marital status as yours; someone whose hair you wished you had; someone who traveled more than 100 miles (160 kilometers) to get here; someone who listens to the same music that you do; someone who speaks a foreign language, etc.

Note: *Create a list that is appropriate to the group. Make it as specific as you can. Include getting-to-know-you questions, as well as simple tasks such as: "Sit in someone's lap for ten seconds"; "Ask someone to sing the first line of 'Yellow Submarine'"; or "Get someone to give you a quarter." "Signatures" allows for instant interaction and familiarity — how many people have you sung to within minutes of meeting them?*

Mask Making

Age Level: 6+

Group Size: 2-20

Activity Level: 5

Location: Inside or outside

Supplies: Plaster cast material (available from craft stores or medical supply stores) cut into 2- to 3-inch (5- to 8-centimeter) strips; small pieces of varying shapes and sizes; Vaseline; vessels to hold water and cast material; plaster, paint, fake fur, feathers, glitter, etc.

Set-Up: Have all supplies assembled and ready for use. The group gets into pairs. You will need a space where half the group can lie down comfortably.

Description: The basic form of a mask is made on each player's face. Partners assist each other in getting the basic form made.

The first partner lies down after tying back any long hair and applying a thin layer of Vaseline to his or her face. After dipping strips of plaster cast material in water to soften them, the second partner applies them to his or her partner's face. Eyes can remain closed (mask will be "blind") or open (carefully mold material around the eyes to leave openings in the mask).

Weak areas should be reinforced with plaster paste or more cast material while the mask is still damp. After masks are thoroughly dry and hard, they can be decorated with paint, feathers, leather, fur, glitter, etc.

Note: *Take great care when working with plaster. Flush eyes immediately with cool water if plaster gets into them. Encourage mask makers to be as creative as they want. Masks often tell quite a lot about their creators, so the sharing of masks can be very meaningful. A play or dramatic presentation can be part of the project. Mask making is suitable for some younger children if there is supervision and guidance.*

Machine

Age Level: 5+

Group Size: 15-40

Activity Level: 3

Location: Inside or outside

Supplies: Cards with the names of several different machines on them; one machine per card. Examples of machines: pinball machine, bowling pin reset machine, washing machine, or food processor.

Set-Up: Divide the main group into smaller subgroups of 4 to 6 players each.

Description: Give each subgroup a card with the name of a machine on it. Using all of its members as parts of the machine, the group must act out the machine. When ready, smaller groups perform in front of the rest of the group; other players try to guess what machine is being performed.

Note: *Each group will need space away from the others in which to create and work together. Allow ample time for group members to act out their machine before you ask for guesses. "Machine" allows players to have input, give ideas, and create together — an excellent bonding activity.*

Would You Buy This?

Age Level: 11+

Group Size: 10-80

Activity Level: 3

Location: Inside or outside

Supplies: A wide variety of unusual packaged products, such as food products, personal items, cosmetic type products, etc. Many such items can be found in a regular grocery store; just look around for unusual packaging or items, and think creatively!

Examples: a jar of pickled pig's feet, cat hairball remover, salmon eggs (for fishing), imitation fishing bait, etc. You will need one item for every four to eight players.

Set-Up: Divide the group into subgroups of four to eight participants. Allow ample space for subgroups to create and practice.

Description: Each subgroup must come up with a commercial to sell its product. However, products should be presented as having uses other than those would have in real life. (Imitation fishing bait, for instance, could be marketed as high fashion jewelry.) Remind participants that they must try to convince others of the value of their product. Anything goes here — creativity is key. Give the group ample time to brainstorm, decide on an idea, practice, and perfect it. When everyone is ready, each subgroup performs its commercial in front of the rest of the group.

Note: *Encourage creativity and group participation. If there are shy, non-acting players, then help the group to find a role that will allow those players to participate. "Would You Buy This?" naturally brings forth humor and a sense of playfulness. Like "Machine," it allows players to have input, give ideas, and create together; it is an excellent bonding activity.*

That's Exactly What It Is

Age Level: 11+

Group Size: 6-12

Activity Level: 4

Location: Inside or outside

Supplies: One strange-looking, preferably unidentifiable object. Examples: a small, shriveled, dried-up apple; a piece of odd plumbing or mechanical part; gel-like fish bait.

Set-Up: The group sits comfortably in a circle; around a campfire is nice.

Description: This game encourages creativity, imagination, and storytelling. The Game Leader starts the game by holding up the object and telling a one- to two-minute story about what the object is. The story should be as interesting, humorous, and outrageous as imagination and good taste allow. The story ends with, "And that's what this is," whereupon the rest of the group echoes in unison, "That's *exactly* what it is!" The object is passed around the circle until all players have a chance to tell their story.

Note: *Often the storyteller lies dormant in us or is shy. This simple game allows individuals to express themselves to the group in a safe, creative way.*

Two Truths and a Lie

Age Level: 10+

Group Size: 6-20

Activity Level: 5

Location: Inside or outside

Supplies: None

Set-Up: The group sits comfortably in a circle; around a campfire is nice.

Description: Ask players to think of two incidents or experiences in their lives that were unusual or hard to believe, or that were scary or funny, or that somehow stand out and make a good story. Then ask them to silently make up a third story.

The Game Leader starts, in order to set an example and get the game going. The Game Leader tells all three of his or her stories — two true incidents and one lie. When the Game Leader finishes, players vote for the story they thought was the lie. When all votes are in, the Game Leader reveals which story was the lie. The next player takes a turn, and so on around the circle.

Note: *Encourage players to make up their lie completely and not just to alter the truth a little. You can keep a tally to see which teller fooled the most people and also which player guessed the most lies. Stories are meant to be brief — we suggest 30 seconds per story. Watch that the stories don't get so long and involved that the rest of the group loses interest. If the group is* *interested in a more elaborate telling of a particular story, that can be a natural extension of the game and can be a valuable way for players to share their life stories. Sharing life stories is an excellent way to deepen friendship.*

Autograph

Age Level: 14+

Group Size: 8-15

Activity Level: 3

Location: Inside or outside

Supplies: 3 x 5-inch (8 x 13-centimeter) index cards; pens or pencils. One card and a pen or pencil for each player.

Set-Up: Give each player a card and a pen or pencil. Ask players to write a question on the card that they would like to ask the members of the group.

Description: When everyone is ready, players circulate amongst themselves and ask one another, "Can I get your autograph?" Players sign their names and answer the question on each other's cards. Answers can be given verbally or written on the card. Players attempt to get as many autographs and answers as possible.

Allow the game to continue until everyone has gotten autographs from at least half of the group. Ask the group to form a circle. The Game Leader begins with the first person on his or her left. "I'd like to introduce Mary." The Game

Leader then reads his or her own question aloud to the group and reads or relates Mary's answer. For example, "My question was 'What is your favorite place on Earth?' Mary's favorite place on Earth is her garden." The Game Leader then asks how many players have Mary's autograph and chooses three or four people to read aloud or relate Mary's answers to their respective questions. Play continues around the circle until everyone has been introduced.

Note: *This game allows for a wide range of risk taking, as each player has the choice to ask a more personal or a less personal question. Encourage meaningful questions that will allow participants to get to know more about each other.*

Spices in the Pantry

Age Level: 4+

Group Size: 2+

Activity Level: 4

Location: Inside

Supplies: Blindfolds for half of the participants. Spices.

Set-Up: None

Description: Players pair up. One person in each pair puts on a blindfold. The seeing partner picks a spice (from "the pantry") and puts a small amount on the blind partner's tongue. The blind partner tries to identify the spice.

Note: *This is a great game to play with family members. It is a trust activity and can be an exciting way to explore new flavors. Special care should be given to the amount of spice that is placed on the tongue, as they can be very strong when not contained in foods. Before proceeding, ask participants to inform you of any allergies they may have.*

Have You Ever?

Age Level: 8+

Group Size: 12-20

Activity Level: 2

Location: Inside or outside

Supplies: One space marker for every player, less one. Space markers can be any flat object that can be stood upon.

Set-Up: The group forms a circle with a comfortable amount of space between players. Give every player a space marker to stand on. The Game Leader begins in the center of the circle to explain and start the game.

Description: Player One (the Game Leader to start) is in the middle of the circle. Player One's objective is to get onto a space marker. In order to do this, he or she must ask a question of the group, beginning with the phrase, "Have you ever…?" Player One completes the question with something she has experienced, done, thought, or felt. For example, "Have you ever traveled to Central America?"

Anyone in the group who can answer "Yes" to Player One's question must move off of his or her space marker and find another. Players *only* move if they can honestly answer "Yes" to the question. Meanwhile, Player One also tries to get onto a space marker. Whoever cannot get onto a marker moves to the middle and asks the next question. Remember that Player One (anyone in the middle) must be able to answer "Yes" to his or her own question.

Note: *Since this game is all about asking questions, it can easily be adapted to most age groups. The purpose of the game is to find out about fellow players and what their common or dissimilar experiences are. Encourage questions that will facilitate* *this, and discourage questions that are so common that the whole group moves but no one learns anything. Questions should be specific, but not so exact that no one else could match the experience directly.*

Encourage players to think of three or four questions ahead of time, so that they are ready if they end up in the center. If a player in the center can't think of a question, he or she can trade places with someone else. Players may take the "none of your business" option and not move spaces. It is the Game Leader's responsibility to ensure that all players have a chance to ask questions and that the center position isn't dominated by a few.

Because questions can be quite personal, or because it is a safe place, players sometimes use the game to reveal difficult aspects of their lives or past; they may be seeking support or understanding. Therefore, it may be necessary (before or after the game) to ask for confidentiality.

M-and-M Sharing

Age Level: 12+

Group Size: 8-30

Activity Level: 4

Location: Inside or outside

Supplies: A bag of M-and-M candies for each subgroup.

Set-Up: Divide larger groups into subgroups of about eight players each.

Description: Ask each player to take as many M-and-Ms as they want (up to 15). Explain that for every M-and-M they take, they will tell the group something about themselves. The Game Leader begins, in order to set tone. After one round, explain that the second round will be for deeper sharing.

Note: *Ensure confidentiality. Make sure players know that what they share is a matter of choice. This game uses a simple device — candy — to help create an atmosphere of sharing one's stories, life experiences, and family life. How much each individual risks and trusts through sharing is an indicator of the group's readiness to risk and trust together. This activity is excellent for deepening friendships through personal sharing.*

Feeding Friend-zy

Age Level: 3+

Group Size: 2-40

Activity Level: 4

Location: Inside or outside

Supplies: Finger food in bowls (fruit, etc.) and caramel dip, OR veggies and dip, OR dried fruit and chocolate dip, OR ice cream and spoons (other combinations also possible).

Set-Up: Divide group into smaller groups of four to six players, sitting close together.

Description: This isn't really a game but it sure is fun! First explain that "Feeding Friend-zy" is a silent activity. The rules are simple: Each group is given two bowls — a bowl of fruit and a bowl of caramel (or other combination). No one may feed themselves, they may only feed another person.

Note: *Feeding another person is a surprisingly intimate activity that few share after infancy. Yet it is a very bonding experience. We have found that keeping silence helps to create an atmosphere* *of giving and caring, rather than one of anxiety or greed. Because participants can't call out, "Me, me, feed me!" they seem to relax and naturally take care of all. You can also try "Feeding Friend-zy" without imposing silence and discuss differences from the silent version. (This is a higher risk activity, as the potential for smearing rather than feeding is high).*

Cooperative Cooking

Age Level: 4+

Group Size: 2-8

Activity Level:

Location: Inside or outside

Supplies: String; duct tape; blindfold.

Set-Up: Your kitchen.

Description: During any meal preparation, eating, and cleanup, tie two cooks together at the wrists with string (leaving one arm free each); or duct tape one or more cook's thumbs to their palms; or blindfold one cook; or have one cook pretend that he or she cannot speak the language of the others. Allow the rest of the group to come up with strategies for fully including everyone and getting the meal prepared.

Note: *This simple variation of a normal life activity can have profound and lasting effects on the participants. Communication is challenged; teamwork is challenged; and relationship is unavoidable. Of course it is the person's choice to take on one of these challenges. Monitor safety and possible conflicts, and spend some time afterward discussing the challenges and the experience.*

If He/She Were a House

Age Level: 13+

Group Size: 12-25

Activity Level: 4

Location: Inside or outside

Supplies: None

Set-Up: Player One leaves so that he or she cannot see or hear the group as it chooses Player Two.

Description: Player One returns to the group and tries to guess the identity of Player Two by asking questions that take the form, "If this person were a ——— (house, animal, type of music, breed of dog, flower, etc.), what kind of ——— would they be?"

Players raise their hands to answer. Player One calls on one player per question to get an answer. After three questions, Player One must make a first guess; after two more questions, a second guess; and after one more question, a third and final guess. If at any time Player One guesses the identity of Player Two, that round is over and a new round begins.

Note: *This game is best played when players can grasp the subtlety and sophistication that is possible. The Game Leader can facilitate this by framing the game carefully: Tell players, when answering the questions, to think of Player Two's personality or character and not his or her likes and dislikes or physical* *appearance. Tell them to take care not to be too obvious but to think about the person and how his or her personality might be represented by the object in the question. For example, for the question, "If this person were a car, what kind of car would they be?" an answer such as, "A Dodge pickup" would convey you one impression of the person, while, "A red Porsche" would convey an entirely different one.*

Monitor the group closely for derogatory or unkind answers. Make sure everyone gets a chance to participate in some way and that the answers aren't dominated by a few. This game is particularly popular with teens, as they are highly interested in what their peers think of them. This game can lead to discussions of identity, personality, and how well they do or do not know another.

Inner Circle/Outer Circle

Age Level: 13+

Group Size: 16-60

Activity Level: 4

Location: Inside or outside

Supplies: A list of questions, formulated ahead of time by Game Leader.

Set-Up: Divide the group into two circles an inner circle and an outer circle so that players are facing each other in pairs.

Description: The object of the game is to stimulate discussion and allow players to interact with each other, especially with those that they wouldn't normally share important dialog with. The Game Leader reads a question aloud. The players in the inner circle answer the question to their partners in the outer circle. The Game Leader allows a set amount of time for answers — usually one to two minutes. At time, the Game Leader announces, "Switch." The other partners then answer the same question. At time, the Game Leader announces, "Rotate." The inner circle rotates one player clockwise. Now each player has a new partner.

The Game Leader begins by asking a second question. This time the players in the outer circle answer first. Continue the game, rotating the inner circle at every new question and alternating between inner and outer circles for who answers first.

Note: *The Game Leader should spend ample time thinking of meaningful, important, and thought-provoking questions that are specific and appropriate to the group.*

INITIATIVES

INITIATIVES OFFER A QUANTUM LEAP in both opportunity and risk compared to the Cooperative Games and Activities. A well-designed Initiative will present numerous decision-making opportunities and call upon a variety of physical skills. In order to complete the task, players must challenge and transcend some habitual ways of relating to themselves and others.

In the Initiatives, no one ability is more important than another, so the status seeking that often occurs when one excels at a particular skill is de-emphasized. Neither the strong tree climber nor the innovative tool user, for instance, is more important than the competent communicator. And the shy introvert often carries the vision that informs others on the skillful use of their talents in best accomplishing the task. Indeed, interpersonal competition or comparison is a hindrance when it interferes with communication or prevents recognition of each person's talents. Yet, even though participants may comprehend the unusual conditions created by the Initiative, it is still often difficult for them to make the adjustments that would allow for a mutually satisfactory completion of the task at hand. The greatness of the Initiative opportunity seems to lie in just this dynamic.

Initiatives also challenge facilitators. Facilitation requires both attention and presence. Interpersonal dynamics reveal themselves in subtle ways and can change in the blink of an eye. Indeed, the most important ones often appear ordinary or habitual and draw little or no attention to themselves, making them difficult to spot. Which participant is most challenged, for instance, and in what way? How do others react? What can be observed about family or group dynamics? In our experience, facilitators who bond with participants while still maintaining the ability to observe behavior with a clear eye are best able to access and maintain the requisite attention.

Facilitators must stay keenly aware of strategizing: the ways in which the group will gather and communicate about its problem-solving approach. Each group is unique, and though there are no hard and fast rules, our experience has been that facilitators need to listen closely during strategizing. For instance, one group may need only a short period of time to decide how it wishes to proceed; another may need considerably longer to come to consensus before it begins an Initiative.

Facilitators also need to be prepared to modify their instructions as circumstances warrant. For example, we have sometimes proposed that a group incorporate in its strategy a rule of silence that will apply to everyone over the age of 25 so that younger participants have a chance to be heard. At other times, we have requested that people communicate with the group using another person as their interpreter: father/daughter, elder/youth, etc. Part of the facilitator's role, then, is to provide leadership to foster learning.

As well as paying attention to framing and debriefing, facilitators must also be sensitive to a variety of other factors as they work: time allocation, reminders about inclusion, hints (at appropriate moments) for accomplishing the task, and safety concerns of both a physical and an emotional nature. Overall, judicious planning and instruction that allow for meaningful learning increase the potential for group bonding among participants and facilitators alike. Facilitation, therefore, is both an offering of oneself and an integral component of a social contract. Without question, the attitudes and capacities that we, as facilitators, bring to the Initiative greatly influence the quality of the participants' experience.

We believe it is very important to support well-being and honor the developmental needs of each participant. As with the rest of the activities in *Win-Win Games for All Ages*, the Initiatives are informed by holism — most specifically by a holistic appreciation of human development known as Natural Learning Rhythms (see About EnCompass at the end of the book). The "Age Level" designator that is part of each Game or Initiative, for instance, arises out of our knowledge of and sensitivity to those learning rhythms and is an attempt to aid facilitators who do not have specialized knowledge of child development.

The Initiatives can be very powerful tools for deepening relationships, and we suggest that you approach them with careful preparation and forethought. Although nothing can substitute for proper training and accurate information, it is not absolutely necessary to have knowledge about and experience with holistic child development in order to facilitate the Initiatives. Such knowledge, however, will certainly enhance and increase your skills in strategizing, communicating, implementing, and debriefing them.

Initiatives can be used in many settings, including the classroom, any recreational situation, in families, and with groups of friends. They are very useful when people meet for a purpose, yet do not know one another well (in camps, youth groups, and support groups). Please refer to the Bibliography for information about additional Initiatives. We wish you all good luck with these Initiatives and believe that once you get started, you will find many ways to incorporate them into your life.

Puzzler

Age Level: 5+

Group Size: 8-30

Activity Level: 3

Location: Inside or outside

Supplies: Homemade puzzles. Take a variety of magazine photographs, paste them onto thin cardboard, and then cut the cardboard into varied shapes and sizes. Make sure you have at least one puzzle piece for each player. Create puzzles appropriate to the age group you are working with by choosing suitable photos and cutting the pieces into less or more complex shapes and sizes.

Set-Up: The group forms a circle.

Description: Ask participants to close their eyes and open their hands. Tell them that the Game Leader will place an object in their hands but that they must keep their eyes closed until the activity begins. Then, with open eyes, they must find their place in the group by matching their object to other like objects.

Variation: To increase difficulty and challenge, make two or more puzzles out of identical cereal boxes, but cut the pieces differently. Or have large groups make one huge puzzle out of a poster; when finished, let participants keep their piece as a symbol that they are part of the whole group.

Framing and Debriefing: This activity can be played silently or with talking. Frame this activity with the theme of finding your place in a group. Use the activity to debrief issues of fitting in, of finding one's place, and of the picture needing every piece in order to be whole.

Note: *This activity can be used as a means to divide a large group into two or more smaller groups. Pass out the pieces to two or more complete puzzles randomly and allow the groups to naturally divide. Use one puzzle of eight to ten pieces per subgroup, for example.*

Moon Ball

Age Level: 5+

Group Size: 6-30

Activity Level: 3

Location: Inside or outside

Supplies: One or more inflatable beach balls.

Set-Up: A large play area.

Description: The group's task is to keep the beach ball in the air for as many hits as possible. No one player may hit the ball more than once before another player hits it (no consecutive hits by one player). If the ball drops to the ground, the count must begin again at zero. Counting begins with the first hit.

Framing and Debriefing: Ask the group how many hits they think they can achieve. Stop the action once the ball drops and allow the group to voice ideas on strategies for including everyone, goal setting, communication, etc. Since it is easy for a group to get caught up in the importance of the external goal — in this case, getting as many hits as possible — "Moon Ball" is a great Initiative for introducing and debriefing concepts such as achievement priorities and relationship priorities. The discussion can then be opened up to consider what other goals the group feels are important and how it can stay connected.

Multitask Race

Age Level: 2+

Group Size: 8-15

Activity Level: 1

Location: Outside

Supplies: You will need a variety of materials for this initiative:

Five-gallon (20-liter) bucket

One suit of cards, Ace through King

One dozen tennis balls, in two different colors

Blindfolds

Several small Frisbees, all different colors

Small ball or toy and a large spoon

Soccer-type ball

Start/Finish line

Stop watch

Other ideas and different supplies can also be used — just use your imagination.

Set-Up: In a defined area, set up as many task stations as you want your group to complete. Avoid tasks that a single person can do alone. Instead, create tasks so that pairs of players must depend on each other and groups of two, three, four, or more players must work together cooperatively. The tasks suggested here are those that can be set up from the foregoing supply list and are suggestions only — you can come up with many more:

- **Cards:** Place the suit of cards face down in a shuffled pile. Place a blindfold near the cards. The task is to put the cards into sequential order. The only player who may touch the cards must be wearing the blindfold, and no one may physically touch the blindfolded person. The task can be carried out in silence or with talking — either is fine.

- **Tennis Balls:** Place tennis balls in a pile at one end of the Multitask area, and place the 5-gallon (20-liter) bucket at the opposite end. The task is to get all the balls into the bucket. One color of balls can be touched; the other color cannot be touched by any player directly or by a player's clothing.

- **Frisbees:** Pile Frisbees far from the bucket. The task is to get all the Frisbees into the bucket. Each player can only touch each Frisbee once. When contacting a Frisbee, that player's feet cannot move.

- **Toy and Spoon:** Place a small ball or toy, a large spoon, and a blindfold far from the bucket. The task is to get the toy into the bucket. The only player who may touch the spoon must be blindfolded. Only the spoon can touch the toy. No one may touch the blindfolded person.

- **Soccer Ball:** Place the ball on the ground, far from the bucket. The task is to get the ball into the bucket. No one may touch the ball with his or her hands

or arms. The ball may not touch the ground. A
minimum of two people must be used to transport
the ball.

Description: This initiative is set up as a race (unless young
children are playing. *See note*). Explain to the group that it
has several tasks to complete as quickly as it can and that it
has three chances to get its best time. Before starting the race,
take the group around to all the tasks and explain the details
and rules that go with each one.

The race begins with everyone behind the Start/Finish
line. The clock starts when the first player of a group steps
over the line and stops when its last player steps back over the
line. Give the group time to strategize and plan before starting each round. Re-set the course after each round.

Framing and Debriefing: Many issues can surface during
this initiative: there is the overall task of getting every mini-
task completed as quickly as possible; there are numerous
sub-problems to solve throughout; and issues of inclusion
and communication are common. Observe carefully. Debrief
the smaller groups' work, as well as the whole group as a unit.
Explore how time pressure and competition affect relationships and communication.

Note: *In groups with members of various ages, such as families,
players as young as two years old can easily participate. In groups
of youngsters — all six-year-olds, for example — it is not necessary or advisable to frame the initiative as a timed race: one
round is usually sufficient.*

*The main safety concern is for blindfolded players. Make
sure that you spot for them and watch for inadequate guiding.*

Steppingstones

Age Level: 5+

Group Size: 5-10

Activity Level: 2

Location: Inside or outside

Supplies: Steppingstones can be improvised out of anything from paper plates to actual stones. You need

flat objects that can be stood on, picked up, and passed from person to person. Plywood circles 18 inches (45 centimeters) in diameter work well, as do carpet squares. You will need about two-thirds the number of steppingstones as you have members of your group (six objects for nine people, etc.).

Set-Up: Establish a start point and an end point in a large area that the group must get across without contacting the ground or floor. Players can only step on the "stones." Make sure the area is large enough so that participants run out of stones before they are across.

Description: The group's task is to get everyone safely across a "dangerous" area, using only the steppingstones. There are not enough stones for every person in the group, so participants must use their resources wisely to get everyone across.

Framing and Debriefing: This initiative emphasizes the essential importance of each group member: the group cannot leave anyone behind; everyone must work together and get physically close in order to succeed in getting all across.

In the debriefing, ask if everyone felt included and if ideas were listened to. Discussion can include topics of inclusion and the notion that everyone matters. Often, children between the ages of five and seven figure out how to better cooperate in this activity than do older children or adults.

Note: *You can tell the group that they must take their whole group in one pass, or see if they decide to take several trips in order to get everyone across. Watch out for players placing stones too far apart for other players to reach easily, and for those making a leap to get to the stone.*

Knots on a Rope

Age Level: 5+

Group Size: 6-9 per rope

Activity Level: 3

Location: Inside or outside

Supplies: 10-foot (3-meter) lengths of 3/8-inch (11-millimeter) rope.

Set-Up: Tie several evenly spaced, single overhand knots in the rope lengths. Use one length of rope per six to nine players. Have players grasp the rope between knots with one hand, spacing themselves evenly.

Description: Players must get the knots out of the rope, without ever moving or taking the one hand off of the rope. They may not switch hands.

Framing and Debriefing: This initiative often brings up issues of competition and separation, because the players at each end of the rope treat each other as separate teams. Explore why this happens in the debriefing. If some players are blindfolded, observe how the blindfolded players are words. If you are playing with families with children over 17 years old, use words like "interconnectedness," "space," "time," "relationship," and "gratitude."

Description: This activity is best played outside, in an environment that has lots of natural objects in it. Give each family a packet. Tell them to find what is written on each card.

Framing and Debriefing: Allow the family to interpret the rules broadly. The Game Leader need only tell the family to find whatever they see written on the card. Finding the object, feeling, or quality may mean finding a tangible symbol, or it may mean offering something intangible. For example, one player may find "love" represented in a flower, while another player may hug someone.

During debriefing, talk about the qualities and objects and what they meant to the player who chose them. Watch family relationships in this activity. Is everyone allowed to choose his or her own objects freely? Is there control or interference? What happens when there is?

Note: *This activity can be played with groups of young people, as well as with families, and works particularly well with children under the age of 12.*

treated. Debrief the experience in relation to the blindfolded players' experience.

Note: *"Knots on a Rope" can be set up as a blindfold initiative, involving either the entire group or part of it.*

Family Scavenger Hunt

Age Level: 3+

Group Size: 2-30, divided into family groups

Activity Level: 2

Location: Outside

Supplies: A small packet of cards with texture, feeling, and quality words written on them. One packet per family.

Set-Up: Create the packets ahead of time, custom-made for each family. Have plenty of cards printed with sensation-based words such as "fuzzy," "sticky," "soft," "icky," "hot," etc. Include feeling words such as "friendship," "trust," "caring," "anger," "happiness," etc. and words that convey qualities such as "freedom," "power," "love," "individuality," "relationship," etc.

Each family's packet should contain cards that correspond to the age/stage of the children in the family. For example, for children younger than 8 years old, use sensation-based words; for 9- to 12-year-olds, use feeling-based words; and for 13- to 17-year-olds, use the quality-based

Nuclear Waste

Age Level: 13+

Group Size: 8-12

Activity Level: 3

Location: Outside

Supplies: A section of rubber bicycle tube with the valve cut out, tied into a circle large enough to fit over a 5-gallon (20-liter) bucket when stretched; six or more 15-foot (4.5-meter) ropes; enough rope or PVC pipe to make a 20-foot (6-meter) diameter circle and a 6-foot (2-meter) diameter circle; one two-pound (one-kilogram) coffee can, three-quarters full of balls; a second coffee can or 1/2-gallon (2-liter) plastic milk jug, full of water; a 5-gallon (20-liter) plastic bucket, with lid.

Set-Up: Using rope or PVC pipe, lay out a 20-foot (6-meter) diameter circle with a 6-foot (2-meter) diameter circle in the center. Place the 5-gallon (20-liter) bucket upside down on the ground, inside the small circle. Put the coffee can, with the balls in it, on top of the bucket. Place all other supplies outside the large circle where the group can get to them easily.

Description: The objective of this initiative is to safely get the can containing the balls ("spent nuclear fuel") inside the bucket ("decontamination box"); the water ("nuclear fuel coolant") into the can; and the lid securely set on the bucket, thus containing the "nuclear fuel" safely inside a double-walled containment chamber, ready for permanent disposal. The only supplies that can be used are the ones provided. No one may touch the area within the circles. Nothing can leave the inner circle until "containment" is achieved; otherwise players may be overexposed to the "toxic waste."

Framing and Debriefing: This initiative requires that the group work with materials to solve a logistical problem. In initiatives of this type, a group's needs are sometimes bypassed in the quest to solve the problem and "be successful." Watch the group carefully. Are they including everyone, even those who are not comprehending the solution? Are all ideas being heard? Is solving the problem a higher priority than the group's cohesiveness or understanding?

Note: *Children younger than 13 years old can participate in this initiative if there are older players as well.*

Dream Bucket

Age Level: 13+

Group Size: 8-12

Activity Level: 3

Location: Outside

Supplies: A section of rubber bicycle tube with the valve cut out, tied into a circle large enough to fit over a 5-gallon (20-liter) bucket when stretched; four or more 15-foot (4.5-meter) ropes; enough rope or PVC pipe to make a 20-foot (6-meter) diameter circle and a 6-foot (2-meter) diameter circle; a 5-gallon (20-liter) plastic bucket; and a 6 x 10-inch (15 x 25-centimeter) cloth or mesh bag, with drawstring for closing.

Set-Up: Using rope or PVC pipe, lay out a 20-foot (6-meter) diameter circle with a 6-foot (2-meter) diameter circle in the center. Place the 5-gallon (20-liter) bucket upside down inside the small circle. Place the bicycle tube and 15-foot (4.5-meter) ropes outside the large circle where the group can get to them easily.

Description: This initiative has two parts. You will need the cloth (or mesh) bag for the first part. Gather the group. Give participants about five minutes to find a natural object, such as a leaf, stone, pine cone, etc., that in some way represents a dream or a hope that they have (when working with families, we add, "for your family"). Players pass the bag around the circle, putting their object inside and telling how it represents their dream or hope. When all the objects are in the bag, place the bag on the upturned bucket in the middle of the circle. Give the other supplies to the group. The second part of the participants' task is to retrieve their hopes and dreams from the "Field of Despair." They must retrieve the entire bucket — not just the bag. They can only use the supplies you have given them. No one may touch the area within the circles.

Framing and Debriefing: The significance of this initiative lies in the value imbued in each player's object. By the time participants have finished describing how the objects represent their dreams, it is clear that the bag holds a precious cargo. The retrieval of the bag, without losing it in the "Field of Despair," becomes paramount. The debriefing can be as much about dreams and hopes as about the group's work in retrieving them.

Note: *Children younger than 13 can participate in this initiative if there are older players as well.*

Magic Carpet

Age Level: 10+

Group Size: 8-30

Activity Level: 3

Supplies: Tarps or blankets cut to size. For a group of 8 to12 participants, the size should be 4 x 5 feet (1.25 x 1.5 meters). For larger groups, cut the tarp or blanket larger accordingly.

Set-Up: Divide larger groups into subgroups of 8 to 12 players each. Ask participants to stand on their "Magic Carpet." Everyone must have both feet on the carpet, with no body parts touching the outside area.

Description: The group's task is to flip the "Magic Carpet" over so that the top is underneath. No body parts can ever touch the floor or ground, and players must stay in contact with the carpet at all times as they fulfill the task.

Framing and Debriefing: "Magic Carpet" requires that problem solving and decision making occur while players are in a physically limited space. Partly because of this limitation, players can fall into a mode of acting on a solution without including or even informing other players of their intentions. Use observations during the debriefing. How could players solve the problem and still include everyone?

Did they make excuses that the space was too confining? What was truly important, and could they recognize and act on it? We live in a busy world where it is often easier to overlook relationship-building communication in favor of expediency and getting the job done. Discuss the values inherent in such choices and how they affect relationship.

Human Ladder

Age Level: 2+

Group Size: 14+

Activity Level: 2

Location: Inside or outside

Supplies: Seven or more 3-foot (1-meter) lengths of 2-inch (5-centimeter) dowels, sanded smooth to eliminate splinters.

Set-Up: Holding the dowels between themselves, and facing each other, players create a horizontal ladder, adjusting the height and space between the dowels to create an interesting climbing obstacle.

Description: While the ladder is held by most of the players, one player at a time climbs the ladder. When the climber gets to the end, he or she takes the place of the last holder, who then starts the climb. The ladder can be extended if the front holders move to the end of the ladder before a climber is through.

Framing and Debriefing: This activity requires concentration and trust, so talk about these qualities before proceeding. Start with the dowels in a pile. Let participants strategize how they are going to arrange themselves and how they will back each other up. Let them decide who is going to hold the dowels and the order in which players will climb. Ask questions, and monitor but do not direct the players — allow them to problem solve and create strategies.

Afterward, debrief the process. This activity invites mutual trust and interdependence, and issues of trust often surface from both the climbers and the dowel-holders. Talk about any struggles, the ways in which they worked together, and what they needed to do to involve everyone.

Note: *If playing with very young children, make sure there are enough older people to maintain safety: young children can hold the ladder but may need a bigger person to help them. Tell climbers to distribute their weight evenly over several rungs, rather than put all of their weight on one. Make sure that holders are strong enough to hold up their end of the dowel for every climber.*

Blind Square

Age Level: 14+

Group Size: 5-20

Activity Level: 3

Location: Inside or outside

Supplies: One or more lengths of ¼-inch or ⅓-inch (9 millimeter or 11 millimeter) rope, generally at least 20 feet (6

meters) long. Blindfolds; one for every player.

Set-Up: Blindfold all players, then hand them the rope and explain the initiative.

Description: The objective of this initiative is to make the rope into a perfect square while being unable to see. When players all agree that they have made a square, they lay the rope down on the floor or ground and tell the Game Leader that they are done. The Game Leader then tells players to take off their blindfolds and observe their work.

Variation: Take the group through a progression before going to the blind square. First ask players to make a circle; allow them to see but not to talk. Then ask them to make a triangle; again, allow them to see but not to talk. Finally, ask them to make a square, allowing them to talk but not to see.

Framing and Debriefing: This initiative requires that players are fairly advanced at keeping communication lines and leadership in sync. It can bring up frustration: groups often struggle with listening to everyone when no one can see.

Debriefing issues can be about listening to all, keeping everyone informed of executed plans, and the stresses of working together without sight.

Note: *This initiative is fairly low-key physically, except for the fact that no one can see. If everyone keeps hold of the rope, it is usually easy to spot and keep everyone safe.*

Egg Drop

Age Level: 8+

Group Size: 4-6

Activity Level: 4

Location: Outside

Supplies: For each group of 4 to 6 players, you will need: one raw egg; 20 plastic straws; 3 feet (1 meter) of masking tape; and a pair of scissors.

Set-Up: If the group is large, divide it into subgroups of 4 to 6 players each.

Description: The objective of this initiative is to create a vessel for the egg so that it remains unbroken when dropped from a height of 8 feet (2.5 meters) onto a hard surface. Give each subgroup a set of supplies, and allow participants to work for a predetermined period of time (20 to 30 minutes) to create their invention. At the end of that time, test each invention by dropping it ceremoniously from the prescribed height.

Variation: "Egg Drop" can be set up as a large-group team effort, with numerous subgroup design teams. If just one design out of many successfully protects the egg, then the whole team succeeds. Each design team must come up with a name for its vessel and must make a pre-drop presentation in which team members explain why they think their design will work.

Framing and Debriefing: If using the variation, careful framing is necessary so that the initiative is set up as a team effort right from the start. "Egg Drop" can easily become competitive. Watch for competition and debrief the issue should it arise.

In subgroups, watch how the decision-making process unfolds: issues of commitment, communication, and competition are common. Because the stakes are relatively high — there is always the risk of the egg breaking (and in fact, most do) — there is increased pressure for the group to succeed. Different people, however, have different values for success and failure. This initiative is especially useful for bringing out those values so groups can examine what success and failure truly mean to each person.

Mind Trap

Age Level: 12+

Group Size: 2-12

Activity Level: 3

Location: Outside

Supplies: Numerous objects such as toys and balls; old household objects such as telephones, telephone books, empty food containers, raw eggs, magazines, beer cans, soda cans, catalogs, etc. A boundary rope long enough to mark an area 15 feet (4.5 meters) long and 10 feet (3 meters) wide. Blindfolds; enough for every player.

Set-Up: Use the rope to set up the boundary area, and randomly place the objects within in. The area should be difficult but not impossible to walk through without stepping on or touching any of the objects; this area is the "Mind Trap."

Description: The group forms into pairs. One partner is the guide; the other is blindfolded. The objective of the initiative is to get the blindfolded players safely through the Mind Trap without stepping on or touching any of the objects. If a player touches an object, he or she must begin again. When one partner is successfully through the Mind Trap, partners switch roles and begin again. Several pairs can go through the Mind Trap at once.

Variation: "Mind Trap" can be used as a whole-group initiative with a slightly different set-up. Make the boundary area a large circle. Make a smaller circle within the larger one. (Rope or PVC pipe can be used for the boundary markers.) Start the group inside the smaller circle. The task is to get every group member out of the danger zone of the Mind Trap and to safety. Every member must be blindfolded as they go through the danger zone. Allow participants to strategize how they can complete this task.

Framing and Debriefing: This activity can be framed by pointing out the objects that can trap our minds and have an impact on our relationships: telephones, food, etc. Ask the group what level of communication may be required for overcoming some of the traps and how our own blindness may contribute to our feelings of being trapped.

Debriefing topics can include partnership, communication, and the effects of distractions and desires. Discussion can range from the general (how as a society we are isolated from each other through distraction) to the personal (how we distract ourselves).

Note: *It is always important to take care when players are blindfolded and to physically protect them when necessary.*

HOLISTIC
LEARNING ADVENTURES

WE HAVE BEEN emphasizing holism and relationship throughout *Win-Win Games for All Ages*. As we have said, the simplest definition of holism is that the whole is more than the sum of its parts and cannot be understood by examining any of its parts in isolation. Rather, the relation ship among the parts, and their synergy, determine the nature of the whole and allow any entity the fullest expression of its essential or ultimate nature — what we call "Ultimacy." Holistic Education takes Ultimacy very seriously, holding it as the *raison d'être* of education.

Most holistic educators believe that Ultimacy plays through each of us in a unique way and that it cannot be defined for another; instead, students must be allowed their own direct experience. Educators, then, are engaged in a delicate, exquisite dance. If a teacher or facilitator creates or comes to a learning situation with a strong agenda about how Ultimacy is "learned," then he or she will not be sensitive to the needs of the student in the moment. In that sense, all curricula should be somewhat suspect. Certainly some curricula create a freer, more open learning climate than do others. However, opportunities for self-actualization are not in the curricula *per se* but in a being-to-being transmission that cannot be taught through verbal instruction. We put ourselves and our students at risk if we invest faith in the curricula rather than in the relationships that allow learning to occur.

81

With these caveats in mind, we present three Holistic Learning Adventures: "What Is a Tree?"; "What Is a Culture?"; and "Wilderness and Wildness." We implement the Holistic Learning Adventures according to the developmental needs of our participants. We are thus able to accommodate a wide age range in the Adventure while (mostly) ensuring relevancy for all. (At EnCompass, we are ready to try working with a single developmental group in a Holistic Learning Adventure. If you wish to know more, email us, and we will be glad to share our work with you.)

Each Holistic Learning Adventure runs for six to eight days. We are fortunate to have a facility where participants can live together during the program. We do not believe that a live-in program is absolutely necessary, though we have not tried to run the program with day students only. If your program must run only during the day, we suggest that you include the nighttime activities in your schedule somehow, since they enhance learning opportunities.

A rather high degree of intimacy — with oneself and with others — is necessary for a learning community to function well, but intimacy develops gradually and cannot be forced. Thus, we design the schedule to address that reality: journaling, for instance, occurs throughout the week and encourages self-reflection and the building of relationship with the self. Games build relationship within groups. We begin with low risk games and activities and then, as the week unfolds, we introduce the higher risk activities that depend on trust between participants. Always we pay attention to the individual nature of the participants and to the unique opportunities of a given moment.

We use six experienced facilitators on a rotating basis for the various learning blocks. Though this arrangement seems to work well, it is by no means perfect, and we continue to explore other options. Guest speakers and relevant field trips can augment and enrich the learning blocks. It is incumbent on each learning group to assess its strengths and weaknesses and choose the facilitation scheme that will work best for its unique needs.

We use at least two facilitators for each activity, preferably one from each gender. Although not always possible, participants of all ages have responded well to this arrangement. We also hold frequent staff meetings, during which we share pertinent information, devise new approaches, discuss the participants' progress, and in general ask for and provide mutual support.

We do not force or coerce participants to engage in any particular activity; neither do we use rewards or punishments of any kind. But we do not let people wander without guidance during a learning block, either. Often we find that reticent or uncooperative participants will stay engaged if they can use a different learning style. For instance, we will encourage someone who is bored by conversation to draw while staying with the group. Or we might switch a participant's learning partner. Sometimes we simply invite a participant to create a response that will maintain his or her connection to the rest of the group. The heart of our approach relies upon relationships between staff and participants and upon creative partnerships for problem solving.

As with any form of cooperative games or activities, facilitators are an indispensable part of the learning community. Their challenge is not to present a curriculum for participants to "learn" but to set up a learning environment in which everyone is invited into opportunities to add to their own self-knowledge. Therefore, it is incumbent upon facilitators and teachers to use a discourse relevant to the learners' respective lives i.e. tailor directions, explanations, and examples to fit the background and experience of the participants. Furthermore, facilitators and teachers must be aware of and able to accommodate a variety of learning styles, be they verbal, mathematical, musical, kinesthetic, spatial, intrapersonal, or interpersonal. And finally, as members of the learning community, facilitators must constantly examine if and how they themselves are deepening and awakening their own self-knowledge.

The holistic view of experiential learning recognizes that experience is an interplay between the inner world and the outer world. It seeks to stimulate intrinsic values, rather than to teach facts, ethics, or moral codes. It accepts each participant as an individual, a member of his or her family, ethnicity, and community. It sees each participant simultaneously as a unique individual and within the context of his or her development moment. It offers one-on-one relationship, as well as relationship in small groups and with the entire learning community. It guides and at the same time offers a free choice of learning partners. No part is isolated; all are accounted for, yet there is no supposition as to the nature of the expression of the synergy of all these parts. When we begin a Holistic Learning Adventure, we never know exactly what awaits, but we do know it will be a real adventure!

What Is a Tree?

The answer we give to the question, "What Is a Tree?" says as much about our own perspective as about the tree itself. Thus, the question suggests a wide open field for learning about trees, about ourselves, and about the way that learning occurs.

This Learning Adventure depends upon presenting the many ways in which trees are perceived by humans. We have used the following categories to devise the activities.

SCIENCES
Biology (ring counts, core samples, weather forecasting, life cycles)
Chemistry
Ecology
Math
Natural complexity
Physics
Relationships (in the tree, tree to forest, tree to environment, tree to historical references, tree to scientific references)
Taxonomy
Time mapping
Trees and fractal geometry

THE ARTS
Art
Fabric
Horticulture
Jewelry

Literature
Paper Making
Poetry
Symbolism
Woodworking (objects of art including totems, masks, sculpture, painting, furniture)

CULTURE
Cities
Economics (raw material to finished product)
History
Religion
Sociology
Vocabulary

EXPERIENCES
Climbing
Human interest stories
Psychology
Walking

When choosing activities, it is best to start with a cornu-
copia of possibilities and then make decisions according to
the needs of participants, staff capabilities, and available
resources. If possible, include an activity from each category,
or choose activities that draw from more than one category
at a time.

Sample Learning Adventure Schedule

There are many ways to organize the schedule and activities
for a Learning Adventure. The sample schedule offered here
is for purposes of stimulation and suggestion. The best
schedule is the one that you create specifically to fit your
context.

Day One

"What Is a Tree?" begins with some Cooperative Games and
Activities and some Initiatives found in this book and in
Everyone Wins. For the evening activity, each facilitator represents one or more perspectives on the way humans perceive a
tree (feel free to dress the part), illustrating his or her viewpoint with a slide show and promoting it with a ten-minute
talk. For instance, one facilitator might take the role of a logger and present slides and facts to support viewing trees as a
commodity and a renewable resource. A second facilitator
might take the position that wood is a medium for art, and
he or she might show slides of jewelry, sculpture, etc. Another
might insist that trees be left just as they are; he or she might
show slides of artists' renditions of treed landscapes, beautiful
trees at sunset, etc. One facilitator represents the philosophical viewpoint. After all presentations have been made, the
"philosopher" moderates a panel discussion that quickly
opens to include audience participation. Thus, in this first
day, the group meets and bonds, receives an overview of the
many perspectives relating to trees, and engages in visual,
auditory, kinesthetic, and dialogical learning.

Day Two

At EnCompass, activities for the morning of Day Two center around a ropes course, while the afternoon learning block draws from the categories of science and culture. We divide the group or keep it as a unit, depending on our resources and needs.

We use the ropes course to give participants an opportunity to increase their self-knowledge. The high course uses ropes, cables, pulleys, and platforms 20 to 80 feet (6 to 24 meters) off the ground, arranged in various configurations. Climbers use a belay system (like that used by rock climbers), and the course calls forth a blend of courage, skill, and trust from participants. The course's low components are closer to the ground. Low ropes activities allow participants to be in and supported by trees while enjoying themselves and developing trust within community. The low course, like the high course, can present an intense challenge to some participants. Both courses demand cooperation and communication. Our facilitation emphasizes observation and communication, not how high, far, or fast participants can go.

If a ropes course is not available to you, use Cooperative Games and Activities along with various Initiatives to provide similar learning opportunities. For high ropes activities, substitute climbing gyms, rock climbing, or a visit to the most spectacular stand of trees in your neighborhood. For low ropes activities, substitute "Hug a Tree," "Tree Silhouettes," "Unnature Trail," "Sounds and Colors" (with trees as a focus), "Indian Log Pass," and "Hunter" (see *Everyone Wins*).

The second principal learning block involves science and culture. They seem naturally connected: science is the child of culture and exists with it in a powerful reinforcing loop. A number of good activities can serve to enrich this learning block. One approach explores the consequences of the burning of wood. How many ways does fire fuel culture, for instance? Would we have human culture as we know it without our ability to create and use fire?

Tell the myth of Prometheus[1] while participants build a fire. If possible, guide them in the use of a fire drill. Have them warm themselves by the fire. Invite a discussion about the value of warmth to their safety and happiness. As a group, inquire into how controlling fire changed the lives of early humans. How might they notice effects of fire other than just its warmth? Throw something light over the fire, perhaps a leaf or some feathers, and watch them rise in the air. Invite the children to begin experimenting with the energy that is released in the heat of the fire. Stimulate creativity by asking what they could do with a tree if they had materials other than those at hand. If needed, show the history of the steamboat. How many other ways has fire been used?

A second approach to science and culture centers around a field trip, in which participants follow the journey of wood from harvest to end use. EnCompass is located near a forest from which trees are harvested, so the process can be picked up at inception and followed to milling. Your locale may offer different possibilities, so find what is available in your area. Interview people involved in the various stages of wood production. (Making videos of the various stages can be particularly creative. Make sure to get permission to tape.) Ask participants to journal at various times of the day. Remind them that journals can include poetry and art. Stimulate conversations about their perceptions, feelings, and insights into culture.

Evenings are good times for quiet reflection. On the evening of Day Two, we tend to introduce the making of spoons or simple flutes (or some other woodcraft) that the children can continue to work on during the week. We do not have fancy woodworking tools on hand, but if you do, a weeklong woodcraft project of some complexity could be very fruitful.

Day Three

We devote Day Three to the history of trees. Trees are ancient, vast, and varied. They are diversity itself. They live in groves, in forests, and alone. Some humans believe they are "standing people." Others believe them to be simply a particular constellation of atoms, molecules, and cells.

But what is their natural history? And how can we find out? How has human intervention shaped that history? Once again, there are many ways to approach these questions as a learning community. Here are some ideas; please do not take them as a lesson plan, or as *the* answer. Indeed, a collective consideration of which activities will serve your inquiry is as important as the activity itself, so don't cheat yourself of the valuable creative opportunity of devising approaches appropriate to your context and group.

An exploration of art is one way to approach history, and it is particularly interesting to examine examples from many cultures. After all, there is no "fact" of history, but simply a record of what some people remember to have happened at a given moment. As art is a unique type of sensitive record, it is a reasonable place to begin. A little library research can unearth a wealth of material. We display various books and leave them available for inspiration.

We like to start by having participants create some art project of their own. Tree art includes wood, rope, collage, bonsai, topiary, and representation.[2] A fine wood instrument is art and also makes music. A collage of the cycles of birth, life, and death of a tree can include the parts of the tree itself. Gentle conversation while or after the children are creating can invite them to self-reflect on their perception of trees and on how that is expressed in their art.

Given their examination of tree art through time and culture and their own experience of creation, what can participants say about the history of trees? What do they wonder about? Size? How trees came to be? What their relationship is with the life around them and the life that depends on them? Any of these questions can be used to explore the natural history of trees. All of them suggest integrated activities that allow opportunities for learning.

We recommend a field trip to a logging site on Day Three, since logging makes the end of a tree's history. There is finality to it. (If you cannot actually go to a logging site, try to visit a mill.) While on site, or soon thereafter, we ask participants to create art again. The difference in their experience of the two art projects makes for excellent self-reflection.

We hold a Council on the evening of Day Three. A format for group communication that we have found quite effective (see the work of Kessler and Zimmerman in the Bibliography), a Council serves the learning community by providing a safe way for people to speak of meaningful and sometime difficult things.

In Council, a nice rock or other special object is passed around the circle. Whoever holds the rock is the speaker; everyone else listens. There is a time limit for speaking and an appointed timekeeper. A topic is introduced, but comments need not necessarily be confined to it. Encourage specific and personal observations.

The leader speaks first in order to set the tone. Participants can pass; if they do, the rock returns to them after having traveled once around circle. After a set number of rounds, usually two, the rock is placed in the middle and anyone can take it and speak.

We try to keep our Council topics to the experiences of the day. That focus often leads to revelations about personal life and important feelings about one another and the Learning Adventure experience. An air of seriousness, leavened with humor, often pervades as the contrasts and complexities of trees begin to become apparent. This use of Council can bring all the experiences of the week into a more coherent focus.

Day Four

On Day Four, we begin to explore the ecology of trees. Who lives in trees and who lives off of trees? What do trees eat and what eats them? Can a forest be composed of trees that are all of one type? Imagine for a moment that all the products now made from wood can be made from other substances. Would trees then have no more value for humans? What exactly are trees worth? These delightful questions point us toward the relationships that trees engender.

We begin the day with periods of observation — both of ourselves and of the trees. What do we see when we take the time to look at the trees? When we use a magnifying glass, a microscope, and binoculars, what creatures do we see living in trees? Why? What do they find there? How does our feeling and thinking change when we discover the day-to-day life of a tree?

We find that journaling and small-group discussions are valuable as we explore our questions about trees, and that Cooperative Games and Activities can help provide kinesthetic learning. Discovery of any sort is often an intimate experience: one can feel amazed, naïve, even humbled as the life of the tree appears. Connections reveal themselves and lead to further connections about all sorts of relationships. Interdependence makes itself known as a generalized actuality, neither abstract nor limited.

Don't forget sound and music. Most people do not account for sound as part of ecology, yet it is as manifestly important as any other phenomena. Listen to the sounds of the trees and to wind through the trees. Is it music? Bring in rhythm and tempo with some gentle music from wooden instruments. Pass around instruments made by native peoples from different continents. Perhaps play some recordings of drums and flutes, or *sakahachi* (from Japan), didgeridoos (from Australia), harps (from Europe), reed instruments (from the Middle East), board zithers (from Vietnam), and other wooden instruments from different cultures. What happens? Remember to ask participants to observe any changes in themselves and their friends when sound and music become the focus.

Here's a game to help children enjoy and understand the life that depends on trees. Children stand in a circle. The Game Leader has a bunch of beanbags or Nerf balls at his or her feet (about two-thirds as many bags as there are children). The Game Leader takes one bag (or ball), catches the eye of any child, and throws the bag. The child who catches it shouts the name of a creature that lives in or on the tree or names something that the tree eats, or that eats part of the tree. That child then throws the ball to another child, who names something different. Play continues until each player has touched the ball once and named something.

In Round Two, the player who began the game takes the ball and throws it to the same person he or she did before, this time calling out what the receiver chose in the previous round. Play again continues around the circle, with the tosser repeating the receiver's original choice.

Introduce another ball, and establish a rhythm so that players become familiar with the pattern. Then introduce as many balls as the group can handle at one time. Soon the creatures in the tree habitat are being named continuously, amid great fun for all.

Another game — "The Web" — is one of our favorites. It is simple yet can lead to very interesting discussions on many topics. In this case, the topic is the life that is in trees. To play, simply take a ball of yarn and wrap a bit around your finger. It is then your turn to speak. Give the most detailed observation that you can of the one form of life you have observed in the tree. Add anything you know (or can guess) about why that life form uses the tree and how it relates to other life forms that share its habitat. Then toss the rest of the ball of yarn to someone else. They do the same as you did, keeping the yarn taut between you. Soon a web forms —one that is analogous to the web of life that exists in the trees.

Be sure to include an exploration of photosynthesis. We suggest a multimedia approach, with perhaps some acting. The level of sophistication depends entirely on the ages and capacities of the participants. We leave it you to fill this out or create something new and different on your own.

The evening is a good time for storytelling. Invite the children to create a story or to describe a memory. Or have small groups create a story together. If stories are read aloud or told, invite the children to work on their woodcraft as they listen.

Day Five

Day Five is all about the esthetics of wood. What makes wood so attractive, anyway? It certainly has nothing to do with production: many of the most expensive wood artifacts have little utilitarian value. Yet our appreciation for wood transcends time and culture, and woodworking has commanded many hours of intense labor. What basic human need, then, is satisfied by wood that has been worked in beautiful ways?

A field trip is an excellent way to explore the esthetics of wood. We begin at a museum that exhibits wood art. We explore books and pictures there and at a well-stocked library. Perhaps we find a museum exhibit of wooden musical instruments. Or a music school might let us come and examine their instruments. There, a teacher might explain how blowing air through wood or strumming taut animal gut on a wooden frame produces such delicious sounds.

We are on the move. Next stop is the home of an artisan who makes wooden instruments. What kind of wood does he or she use? Why? How does he or she choose and treat it? Hopefully many of the children can have the chance to participate in some aspect of instrument creation. Perhaps we will be able to visit a jewelry maker who uses wood as a medium.

Now we take time to journal. As the children work, we gently remind them to record their feelings and impressions from the experiences that they have had so far. We ask them to speculate in their journals about the value of an esthetic endeavor and why wood is so attractive a medium.

If we have musicians in our group, we ask them to play their instruments. If there are dancers, of any age or skill, we ask them to dance the trees, the forest, or the music that they feel. Sometimes we read relevant poetry and let the children draw, dance, and play music as we read. Or we find some trees and play "Hug a Tree."

If there is more time in this day, we might explore wooden weaponry. Often, as with swords and arrows, the weapon maker makes a significant esthetic investment in the weapon itself. Why? Does it make it more effective?

If we think it will be worthwhile, we might hold a second Council in the evening — perhaps including an opportunity for some "tree humor."

Day Six

On Day Six we become philosophers as we seek to understand all that we have done throughout the week. What does it all mean? Why have we done it? Who is right: the logger, the jewelry maker, the artist, the scientist, the biologist, or the poet? All of them? None of them? What happens to the life that is cut down along with a felled tree? Does it matter? What have we learned about ourselves in our exploration of the different trees? What is a tree, anyway?

We often climb a tree together to bring out the philosopher in everyone. You might find it a useful activity, too. The idea is to get everyone up in the tree and seated comfortably and safely. Once there, you may want to simply hang out together. Ask some children to read from their journals or invite someone to play an instrument. Bring some poetry. Inquire into all offered topics. Use noninvasive questions to try to find the root meaning of a "statement" (we have put the word "statement" in quotes, since it can refer to a drawing or song as well as to words). Refer to experiences from the week to deepen the conversation. Challenge older children about which view of trees is correct. Most likely the word "correct" or "right" will be scrutinized. The children will make a connection to intrinsic values if they are able to self-discover how they arrive at whether or not a given perspective is the right one.

Any and all of you can describe what has changed for you during the week. Does anyone know what a tree is? Does anyone know more about themselves and the way they view trees? Could we have culture if we did not have trees? What might it look like? Is our culture expressed through the way we relate to trees?

We devote the rest of Day Six to Cooperative Games and Activities that allow closure. Some good choices are "Still Photograph," "Nature Sculptures," "Team Tag," and "Save the World" (see *Everyone Wins!* for some of these). We have the children complete any woodcraft projects and get them to finish their journals. We may hold a Council to discuss the topic, "What do you wish to say by way of making closure?" The children then pack up and get ready to go home.

Notes

1. Prometheus (Greek mythology) was the Titan who stole fire from Olympus and gave it to mankind. Zeus punished him by chaining him to a rock, where an eagle gnawed at his liver. Hercules finally rescued him.

2. "Bonsai" refers to a dwarfed ornamental tree or shrub grown in a tray or shallow pot. "Topiary" refers to shrubs clipped or trimmed into decorative shapes, especially of animals.

What Is a Culture?

The more we searched for an answer to the question "What is a culture?" the more elusive it seemed to become. Each component of a culture — its economics, religions, ethnic diversity, nationalism, literature, recreation, science, and technology, etc. — is, in itself, a dynamic and complex process. To understand the multitude of combinations and the way each influences and determines culture at any given moment could only be approached, we believed, through experiencing it. Of course, we all experience culture every day. But like fish in water, we seem unaware of the medium through which we move. So the question became: how can we experience culture consciously? In response, we created this Holistic Learning Adventure.

Overview

"What Is a Culture?" is a weeklong experiential exploration of the fundamental components of culture. We use simulation to bring about some of the multiple dynamics and interactions that can exist within and between differing cultures.

At the beginning of the week, we divide participants into two or more "cultures," each with its own particular characteristics and customs. We meet each child individually and privately and provide him or her with some ground rules and a set of Primary Characteristics for his or her culture. Day One and Day Two are set aside for the children to determine to which culture they belong. At the end of Day Two, the different cultural groups are identified, and we hand out a list of Complex Characteristics and a list of Cultural Resources for each. Then, for the rest of the week, the children carry out an assigned set of activities, acting always in accordance with the characteristics and customs of their particular culture.

Participants have the opportunity to fully experience their own culture's ethos and to interact with people who have a different one. The design of the Learning Adventure builds in the potential for children to experience the delight of learning how to honor each other. It also provides opportunities for them to confront and learn about bias and prejudice, since many of the characteristics and customs of one culture conflict with those of another. Similarly, in deciding how they are going to handle their culture's available resources, the children confront and explore ways to address one of the sources of conflict within and between cultures.

Assigning a Culture

All participants in "What Is a Culture?", including facilitators, are assigned to a culture. Before the children arrive, facilitators decide on the characteristics and customs of each culture. Facilitators undertake to model and role play the ones that apply to their assigned culture in order to increase authenticity and to normalize the activities of the Learning Adventure. Then, when the children arrive, we meet each one individually and privately and provide the following information:

1. You are part of a culture that has certain characteristics.

2. You are to express your culture's characteristics in every activity, including meals, bathroom breaks, unstructured social time, tent time, etc.

3. You are supposed to figure out who else is part of your culture by looking for others who express characteristics similar to yours.

4. Even if you spot others who act like you do, you are not to speak about it or approach the person on the subject.

5. There is more than one culture, but you are not going to be told how many more.

6 The facilitators also belong to a culture, perhaps even the same one as yours.

7. You are not to reveal your characteristics to anyone else.

8. If you have any questions, you can privately ask any facilitator but not another participant.

Primary Characteristics

During the assignment process, we tell each child which Primary Characteristics apply to his or her culture. The child must then embody those characteristics during Day One and Day Two.

Here are examples of Primary Characteristics for two cultures.

Culture A:

1. Don't look another person in the eye or face until after two interchanges in a communication.

2. Nonchalantly comment on another person's appearance after the two interchanges.

3. Always clear your throat slightly before speaking.

4. Hold your knife in one hand and your fork in the other when eating. Do not drop the knife and then switch the fork.

5. Regard all space as communal space, except for the bathroom. In the bathroom, be very shy.

6. Always be on time, even if you have to abruptly end an interaction.

Culture B:

1. No left-hand contact with other people or with food.

2. Never talk about someone who is not in your immediate presence.

3. Always address anyone over the age of 25 as Sir or Ma'am.

4. When you are listening to someone, always lower your eyes and nod your head slightly.

5. Always verbally greet people as you pass or meet them.

6. Whenever your body is in contact with water, make a positive comment on how it feels.

Once the Primary Characteristics are assigned, Day One and Day Two are given over to Cooperative Games and

Activities, Initiatives, journal writing, and perhaps crafts and music.

One-on-one meetings regularly occur between children and facilitators. The children often find things difficult at first and need encouragement to remember their roles. Many enjoy watching the other children role play but seem to have a harder time embodying their own culture's characteristics. Meetings help the children to adjust.

We also encourage the children to self-observe. Holistic Education, as you may recall, holds self-observation as a crucial aspect of learning. Therefore, we engage the children in a great deal of inquiry and exploration to help them see how they approach self-observation. Often facilitators and children will mutually design various experiments to strengthen self-observation skills and practice.

At the end of Day Two, the whole group gathers. The time for declaration has come: How many groups are there? Who is in which group? There is no one method for revealing cultures, though our favorite is to invite everyone to help decide what form the declaration will take. Usually, some children want a secret ballot; others want facilitators to announce the correct answer. Some want each person to name the characteristics he or she has seen and to name who has manifested them. Others want to close their eyes and have facilitators place people in their appropriate groups, before being told to open their eyes for the surprise.

Complex Characteristics

Once all the cultures are identified and the children know to which group they belong, we introduce the Complex Characteristics and move on to the next stage of the Learning Adventure.

Here are examples of Complex Characteristics for two cultures.

Culture A:

1. You live on the edge of the forest. Although your people inhabit both the forest and the city bordering it, overall you are the forest people. Trees are alive, and they are the spirits of your elders. To use the trees is to honor them.

2. Everyone dreams of creating an ongoing sustainable relationship to the forest. On the other hand, everyone loves the products of the forest. It is considered an honor to use all parts of the forest, for then they become you.

3. Your culture believes that forest colors are the most beautiful. Art always refers to something about the forest. The most popular areas of a city have the most forest products in them. Places of worship reflect the forest. However, your culture does not believe that vegetables and animals are gods.

4. All your business interactions within your group are cooperative. However, your play is highly competitive, though sportsmanlike.

5. It is rude to lie to anyone. It is also a loss of face to interact with another culture and not get the better of the deal.

6. If you eat the food of another culture, make quiet grimaces and disparaging comments.

7. Whenever possible, refer to the forest to make your point. This may be done using analogy or by pointing out a particular feature of forest life. For example, you might describe snoring by referring to a frog's noise by the pond at night; you might describe change by talking about how the forest reflects the different seasons.

8. Always verbally agree to all the rules of any activity, but in some quiet way and at least once an hour, make up something of your own that violates the rules. Your culture considers such actions creative.

9. Treat people younger than you and that are not part of your group politely, but do not value their opinion. Be nice with them but not real.

10. Never eat alone, even if you have to eat with someone from another culture. The more people at your meal, the merrier. Meals are for talk, eating, and lots of socializing.

11. Always greet members of your cultural group with some sort of touch with your left hand. Do not do this with anyone else. The more ways you do this, the more creative your culture believes you to be.

12. Salute people with whom you feel especially close by waving your hands together over your head for an instant.

13. Never put down a member of your group in front of any member of another culture.

Culture B:

1. You live on the edge of an ocean, and the ocean is the source of wealth. Your culture is organized around conquest and the accumulation of material goods and wealth.

2. Everyone dreams of going great distances to conquer unknowns and gain wealth. Having the opportunity to go on a quest or adventure where you do not know the outcome is considered a great honor. All who have done so are looked at as being closer to the Gods.

3. Your culture believes that ocean colors are the most beautiful. Art always refers to something about the ocean. Places of worship reflect the ocean, and you believe that all Gods come from it.

4. Business is always competitive. At the end of a deal, even if you have made the greatest bargain ever, bemoan how much it is costing you and how poor you are.

5. You are competitive and dominating. It is expected that you will do anything in your power to gain wealth, including lying, but you would never cheat or steal from anyone.

6. If you eat the food of another culture, be overly effusive in your compliments, to the point of being false.

7. Describe everything in terms of the ocean's qualities: flowing, vast, tidal, teeming with life, etc. The best food is ocean food. Very successful people are heavy and eat enormous amounts of seafood.

8. Your religion myths are based on Monsters and Gods. The Monsters devour and take away, and the Gods bring or give great wealth.

9. Refer to everything good in terms of a gain. For example, if you have a baby, talk about how rich this baby will be and how it will help your family to get richer.

10. Emphasize the individual person during mealtime and all other social "hang out" times, when face to face, etc.

11. When greeting people within your culture, wiggle your right hand in the air, as if it were a fish swimming, and verbalize a "shhhhhhh" sound.

12. Always greet people with whom you are especially close by rubbing your fingers together as if you
had a big wad of money between them.

Cultural Activities

Each culture typically spends Day Three organizing itself.
Cultural groups are given a list of activities to be carried out
during the rest of the week, and they have to decide how they
are going to engage with them. Five activities are sufficient,
and we caution against trying to accommodate more.

The list might look like this:

1. Each culture will host a dinner and celebration
    for the others.

2. Each culture will be given resources: a stash of
    snacks and art materials different from those of
    the others. Trade can be encouraged if you wish.

3. Each culture will create an origin myth and then
    read it aloud or perform it for the others.

4. Each culture will design and host a recreation
    afternoon.

5. If it is deemed necessary, each culture shall send
    two representatives to a forum to discuss matters
    of mutual concern, whether they are about mutu-
    al support or grievances.

This list is not exhaustive, and the participants are certainly
welcome to modify it if there is mutual consent to do so.

Cultural groups spend each morning by themselves,
preparing for the joint activity of the afternoon. They, of
course, have to engage the politics of their organization and
then the politics of the interactions. Participants often
arrange such things as self-governance and the allocation of
resources; they may appoint ambassadors and examine and
monitor trade (sometimes scrupulously), constructing

identities to fulfill each role. One culture appointed a scribe to record their interactions and document their creation myth.

Status becomes important, and the bringing of honor to one's culture is a sought-after experience. Conflict may well develop within and between cultures. In short, the simulation brings forth the values and concerns of the culture and is thus well on its way to fulfilling the requirements of a Holistic Education experience.

You may want to invite guest speakers from various other real-life cultures to spend an hour or so each morning with participants to tell stories about what living in their culture is like. The people we invited felt they were met with respect and interest and reported that the participants asked many interesting questions.

Promoting Awareness

Promoting an awareness of self and process is an important part of this Learning Adventure. Again, journaling can be very useful. Frequent private conversations between facilitators and participants also have great potential for promoting awareness; these, however, must be handled carefully so that they allow children the joy of self-discovery. Small-group discussions work well, and the last day of the "What Is a Culture?" Learning Adventure can be profitably used for large, and perhaps even whole-group, dialog.

Here is a list of questions and ideas that facilitators can use to help children to become aware of themselves as cultural beings. (The questions are meant only as a beginning and to stimulate your own creativity.)

1. Did you know how many cultures there were? How?

2. Did you know who was in your culture? How?

3. Are these your typical ways of observing?

4. Are you satisfied with your observational abilities? If not, what experiments might you engage to learn more about observation?

5. What angered you during the week? Why? How do you know when you are angry? Can you trace it to its earliest beginnings in you? (This sequence can be used with any emotion and is best rooted to a direct experience that occurred during the week.)

6. Why did you choose the role you did within your culture? Were you happy with your choice? Did it turn out the way you wanted it to? What would you change? How would you change it?

7. Who have you made friends with? How did it come about? Do you have friends in the other culture(s)? Has anything changed in your feelings towards them during this week? Do you perceive any changes in them?

Feedback

Many of the children reported that they learned about the value of friendship during this Learning Adventure. One child, who had been appointed ambassador for his culture, expressed regret over his actions during a difficult trade negotiation. Many children stated that friendship and group unity were more important than cultural identity and food trades.

Here is some feedback we received after the course was completed.

> *My son came home so open and available to whatever came his way. He noticed when things were not going well for him, and he talked about it. He was different in a very positive way. He could see a problem or a conflict and not feel badly about it.*
>
> — A parent

I liked the trading and the celebration; although we were so different, we had similarities too.
— A participant, in the closing circle at the end of the course

I loved watching people create their cultures. People were really excited and I watched everyone learn as they got more and more engaged. Thank you all. — A facilitator, in the closing circle at the end of the course

Wilderness and Wildness

"Wilderness and Wildness" is the riskiest of the three Holistic Learning Adventures described in this book; it is also the one for which a holistic appreciation of child development is most useful. Its intent is to explore the relationship between wilderness and wildness, both in the world and within oneself. Opportunities for participants to increase their self-knowledge are extraordinary, and facilitation requires careful sensitivity. Therefore, we recommend that you use this Learning Adventure only with children and staff with whom you are somewhat familiar. If you are not familiar with holistic child development, we suggest that you work with one age group at a time and modify the directions accordingly.

Council plays an important role in this Learning Adventure (see "What Is a Tree? or refer to the Bibliography and the works of Kessler or Zimmerman for information on Councils). Council provides a safe forum in which children can share their beliefs about wilderness and wildness and discuss their knowledge, concerns, and expectations of the course. We return to Council regularly during the week in order to provide grounding for the electric-like energy that is often released in "Wilderness and Wildness."

Rationale for "Wilderness and Wildness"

Transpersonal psychology as well as Holistic Education theory holds that to truly know ourselves, we need to connect to our wildness. Some theorists have even made the argument that many of our personal and social ills, including discrimination, pornography, and rampant consumerism stem in part from our lack of connection with wildness, both within ourselves and with the natural world. Yet, history shows that civilization consistently rejects wildness.

There seems to be a belief that people in touch with their wildness cannot be trusted to conform to the mores necessary to maintain civility. American culture certainly seems to endorse this view. We, however, along with many others from the disciplines of psychology, philosophy, medicine, and the arts, disagree. Our work has shown us that the repression of wildness leads to personal and societal ill health. Also, our direct experience of our own wildness has revealed to us that not only is it extraordinarily vivifying, it is also entirely trustworthy. It is actually the suppression of wildness that makes one untrustworthy.

We must make a distinction here between wildness and rebellion. Wildness refers to that which is unconditioned and unconditionable and, therefore, not in any way predictable. Rebellion, on the other hand, is an act or show of defiance against some form of authority or convention; for psychologists and some educators, more often than not rebellion is understood as a compensatory response to the wound of forced and unnatural conformity.

Most children understand what is meant by "wildness," and their experience of it has nothing to do with rebellion. Rebellion is full of tension, anxiety, and distrust. When asked about wildness, teens will often talk about an experience of feeling powerful and free. Their descriptions (which we ask for at the beginning of the Learning Adventure) refer to clarity of the senses, a "knowing" of what was going to happen, and a sense of strength and timing that seems easy and natural (even in challenging situations). These are the very qualities of awareness that we work with in "Wilderness and Wildness."

Day One

After introductory Cooperative Games and Activities — usually including some physically challenging ones — we hold our first Council. At its end, we inform participants that they have the first four days of the Learning Adventure in which to create a personal challenge that will bring forth their wildness.

Participants can work individually or in a group, and the staff is available to help them design and execute their challenge. If participants do not approach the staff, then the staff will approach them to make sure that plans are progressing. In such cases, if participants are not comfortable with the person who contacts them or if a challenge needs a specific type of support, then they are free to choose an alternative staff person with whom to work.

On the evening of Day One, we present age-appropriate movies about wildness. Afterward, we allow time for a carefully supported discussion. Questions to be explored include: Why does this movie evoke a sense of wildness? What did you notice about yourself during this movie? Do you think that others had the same reaction?

Since everyone's mores are different, we have not recommended specific movies in this book. However, we do maintain a list of movie possibilities on our website (www.EnCompass-NLR.org), and we will be happy to answer emails if you are confused about choosing appropriate movies (connection@EnCompass-NLR.org).

Day Two

On the morning of Day Two, we incorporate some competitive games into the design of the Learning Adventure — a teaching strategy that makes "Wilderness and Wildness" unique in our practice of Holistic Education. Though in general we believe that competition between and comparison of children damage initiative and creativity, under certain conditions they can have the beneficial effect of evoking extra effort. In this part of the Learning Adventure, we deliberately intermix cooperative and competitive activities and then invite the children to self-observe in each. As always, our aim is to foster the deepening of self-knowledge. Questions may include: How did your experience of cooperation and competition differ? What did competition bring forth? Is competition necessary to wildness, or does it help access wildness? What did it do to your relationships with others? Is there a correspondence between our relationships and wildness?

On the afternoon of Day Two, several activities take place simultaneously. We offer mask making and body decorating, play loud tribal music, and read literature — *Dr. Jekyll and Mr. Hyde* being a favorite. Participants look through magazines containing pictures of everything from the elaborate tattoos of South Pacific tribes to mountain climbers who have scaled Everest to monks who live silently in caves through their whole lives. We examine featured religious costumes, which often leads to discussions on death and the wild responses that many have to its inevitability.

That night, we take a field trip, hiking into the forested wilderness. At times, we ask for complete silence and invite participants to sit completely still. What can they hear? What do they observe about themselves? How do they recognize fear when it arises? What do they do with the fear?

Late in the night, we organize a game of 'Hunter" (see *Everyone Wins*) and then hike back. In our experience, pushing participants past tiredness helps them to access wildness; pushing to exhaustion only brings unnecessary strain. Knowing that, we carefully plan the route of the field trip so that the hike out is fairly long and the hike back is relatively short.

Day Three

Day Three's activities move participants deeper into the exploration of wilderness and wildness. Everyone sleeps in a bit, and then participants work in their journals. We also hold a Council. (This sequence seems to allow for maximum self-reflection upon the events undertaken thus far.)

At the end of the Council, we announce that chicken is on the menu for dinner and that together we are going to kill and prepare them. Most participants have never slaughtered an animal, and our announcement usually creates a very tense moment. Only those who in some way participate in the actual slaughter of a particular chicken will be allowed to its meat, and vegetarians are exempted from the killing (if they wish to be), since they do not depend on meat for nourishment. Instead, when the time comes, they and a few staff members will go out and gather wild herbs and edible vegetation. Our announcement marks the beginning of an open circle discussion on the subject of killing in order to live.

The morning discussion, activities around the slaughter, and surrounding events take up the remainder of the day. Almost all children seem to respect that life is to be taken to support life, and those who participate in the slaughter often develop elaborate rituals to honor the animal giving its life. Some children choose to protest and demonstrate; some quietly form a mourning circle; others engage in a self-designed sacred ceremony to honor the chicken's life. Sometimes children object so strongly that they become vegetarians on the spot.

That evening, the campfire conversation is alive! The debate can be quite intense as children try to integrate their experience. Fundamental values get challenged and assumptions about such things as friendship, diet, and lifestyle come up for reexamination. We've seen children express an interest in learning more about what it would take to survive in the wilderness. Others become interested in the ways chickens are farmed, the differences and similarities between killing a mosquito and killing for food, whether or not vegetables feel anything when they are harvested, and (most often) the "right" way to approach killing an animal for food.

Day Four

On Day Four, we go exploring the wild side of our immediate environment, building in time for solitude, silence, self-reflection, journaling, and discussion. In a city, activities can include visiting places such as a skyscraper that's under construction, an impoverished neighborhood, places where large amounts of money or commodities of some sort change hands quickly, the bowels of the underground subway system, a slaughterhouse, etc. In rural environments, the whole vast expanse of nature is an invitation to wildness.

Whether we are in the city or the country, the keyword here is "explore" — not as spectators but as direct participants. Can some of the group go up to the top of the skyscraper construction, for instance? Can they help handle the thousands of pounds of fish as they are unloaded at the fish market? Can we spend the night in a shelter, or walk through the cells of a jail? Walk the docks of the shipping lines? What wildlife are we likely to encounter in the countryside around us? What would it be like to sleep out under the stars? In other words, how can the visit bring the wildness inherent in the site and situation into sharp relief? All environments have wildness in them. It is up to the facilitators to bring it to the attention of the participants.

If it is feasible, we sometimes find it valuable to take participants to an environment completely different from the one to which they are accustomed. Or we add some spice to Day Four by doing something incongruous as we explore: reading Thoreau inside a stock exchange or Keats at a slaughterhouse, for instance.

During the late afternoon and into the evening of Day Four, we hold a powerful exercise known as a sweat. (We are fortunate to have a sweat lodge, modeled on a Native American design, but saunas can work just as well — even one in a local health club, if you can use it exclusively for a few hours.) Heat is a powerful purifier and calls forth something quite special if we stay attentive during our time in it. The facilitator must gauge the capacity of participants, but we generally do three 45-minute rounds, with a 5-minute cold dunk or shower in between each round. During each round, we present a "wild" topic and hold a mini-Council. Topics might include death, prejudice, love, family, war, sex, fear, conditioning, drugs, or nature. Both the topic we choose and the way we present it are developmentally sensitive. [There are chapters devoted to doing developmentally sensitive Rites of Passage in both *Natural Learning Rhythms* (Celestial Arts, 1993) and *Rites of Passage: Stages of Life* (M.S., 2000)].

The sweat continues on into the evening, and we find that the heat tires most people out. So instead of continuing any evening discussion before bedtime, we ask participants to pay special attention to their dreams and to write in their journals as soon as they wake up.

Day Five

The morning of Day Five, which will probably start later than usual, centers on self-reflection and expression. Participants are free to choose their medium. We provide plenty of art materials, and those who wish can play music. Many participants will probably continue journaling. Some may want to take part in private, small-group or whole-group discussions.

Personal challenges begin on the afternoon of Day Five. Most likely, for some participants, the planning they have been doing all week has been an obsession; for others, a tangential interest. Now, staff members work with each participant, helping to bring plans to fruition.

One of the week's goals has been to allow participants to experience activities that challenge their sense of the status quo. Keeping safety in mind, staff should be prepared to invite children to look deeply at what they need to do to reach a new understanding of themselves and their world. How can they recreate the world so that their interaction with it teaches them something about wildness?

Here are some of the challenges participants have created. (In each case, we provided suitable "safety nets.")

- A 14-year-old boy spent the entire night secured in the top of a tree.
- A 12-year-old girl made exact plans to visit her biological mother. She completed all the complicated arrangements in camp and executed them upon leaving.
- A shy 13-year-old girl chose to tell true autobiographical campfire stories.
- A 13-year-old boy chose to make three new friends in camp from some of the kids who had been teasing him.
- A 15-year-old boy chose to be brutally honest for a day, no matter what he had to say to anyone.

- A 10-year-old boy fasted through breakfast and climbed up to the top of a tall tree (on belay).
- A 13-year-old girl did a role play about speaking with her mother when her mother gets angry with her.
- An 11-year-old boy fasted for 24 hours, during which he spent 2 hours solo in the forest.
- A 14-year-old boy spent the night sleeping solo in the woods.
- A 14-year-old girl led a discussion based on these three questions: Has anyone been teased before? Has anyone been told that they were stupid before? How many of you believed it?
- A 16-year-old boy spoke with his mom, facilitated by staff, about his true feelings. He had never done this before, because he said he did not trust her.
- A 17-year-old boy spent 2 hours alone in a dark, silent cave.

Day Six

Challenges often extend into Day Six. As participants complete their challenges, they spend a significant amount of time integrating their experience through silent alone time, journaling, or gentle inquiry by a caring adult.

When all challenges have been completed, we hold a Grand Council (with no set time limit) to provide an opportunity for participants to speak about whatever needs to be shared, integrated, or witnessed. The Grand Council concludes the "Wilderness and Wildness" Holistic Learning Adventure.

Feedback

Here is a sample of comments from our closing circle that will give you a feel for the participants' sentiments at the end of "Wilderness and Wildness."

Watching my friend stay in the net in the tree for two hours and everyone overcoming their fears made me feel cool.   — A 16-year-old

During the chicken killing, everyone had a lot of bravery and I want to thank you all. I was the first one to take a chicken's life, and it was so powerful to look into its eyes and say, 'Thank you for letting us have your life.' It reinforced my beliefs, and it made me sad that I don't do that more. Thanks to everyone. Also, it was very powerful for me to sit in the cave for two hours with just me and my mind, no outside sound.   — A 17-year-old

It was inspiring for me to watch my friend be brutally honest for a day as his challenge. The whole week was so wild. I'm re-entering my life without knowing what's going on and that's OK — just not knowing is meaningful.   — An 18-year-old

When we went to Malakoff Diggins that night I was scared. I overcame my fears of dogs and being alone in the wilderness, and I actually slept out alone for a whole night. That's cool. — A young teen

I am blown away by each person's choice of personal challenge, and also how people supported each other. Being in a situation where I was supposedly being a facilitator and with my own experience at the same time, the energy got more and more intense this week, and I was going through the whole process of opening with all of you and learning how to co-lead within that context. I am having feelings of happiness and gratitude to all of you.
                      — A staff member

CONCLUSION

We have just come from another day of participating in Cooperative Games, Activities, and Initiatives with a group of children — this time a fourth grade class from our local public school. Tired, though still somewhat exhilarated, we debrief among ourselves. We try to see areas in which we can improve and, of course, there are many. Yet as we slowly go over the day sharing details, observations, and perceptions, one fact reverberates: we have learned even more about children, about ourselves, and about relationship.

The games and activities create a genuine equality that participants get to experience directly — and that is their power. This equality is not legislatively imposed to mitigate prejudice based on gender, skill, or IQ. Neither is it designed to share power. Rather it is a natural equality, born out of the relationship among participants and their desire for challenge, fun, and goodwill. And by providing a whetstone upon which to hone our capacities, the games and activities satisfy our very human need for personal fulfillment. As one boy said as his team raced toward the finish line, "We did it! We helped Mary untie the knot. Let's go!"

We sincerely hope that the Cooperative Games and Activities, Initiatives, and Holistic Learning Adventures we've presented here will help you and the groups you work with explore and celebrate the diversity and commonality which both differentiate and bind us all.

BIBLIOGRAPHY

Cain, James Hallie, and Barry Jolliff. *Teamwork and Teamplay: A Guide to Cooperative, Challenge, and Adventure Activities That Build Confidence, Cooperation, Teamwork, Creativity, Trust, Decision Making, Conflict Resolution, Resource Management, Communication, Effective Feedback, and Problem Solving Skills.* Kendall/Hunt Publishers, 1998.

Fluegelman, Andrew. *The New Games Book.* Dolphin Books, 1976.

Fluegelman, Andrew, and New Games Foundation. *More New Games! — and Playful Ideas from the New Games Foundation.* Dolphin Books/Doubleday, 1981.

Forbes, Scott H. *Holistic Education: An Analysis of Its Intellectual Precedents and Nature.* Unpublished doctoral dissertation. University of Oxford, 1999.

Kessler, Rachel. *The Soul of Education: Helping Students Find Connection, Compassion, and Character at School.* Association for Supervision and Curriculum Development, 2000.

Luvmour, Josette, and Ba Luvmour. *Everyone Wins!: Cooperative Games and Activities.* New Society Publishers, 1990.

———. *Natural Learning Rhythms: How and When Children Learn.* Celestial Arts, 1993.

————. *Tiger by the Tail: Essays on the Inherent Spirituality of Natural Learning Rhythms.* EnCompass Press, 1998.

————. *Rites of Passage: Stages of Life.* Unpublished M.S., 2000.

Rohnke, Karl. *The Bottomless Bag Again.* 2nd ed. Kendall/Hunt, 1994.

————. *Cowstails and Cobras: A Guide to Ropes Courses, Initiative Games, and Other Adventure Activities.* Project Adventure, 1977.

————. *Silver Bullets: A Guide to Initiative Problems, Adventure Games, Stunts, and Trust Activities.* Project Adventure, 1988.

Rohnke, Karl, Steve Butler, and Project Adventure. *Quicksilver: Adventure Games, Initiative Problems, Trust Activities, and a Guide to Effective Leadership.* Kendall/Hunt Publishers, 1995.

Rohnke, Karl, and Project Adventure. *Cowstails and Cobras II: A Guide to Games, Initiatives, Ropes Courses, and Adventure Curriculum.* Kendall/Hunt Publishers, 1989.

Zimmerman, Jack M., and Virginia Coyle. *The Way of Council.* Bramble Books, 1996.

ABOUT THE AUTHORS

Josette and Ba Luvmour, M.A. are directors of EnCompass: Josette serves as the Family and Adult Program Director, and Ba serves as the Executive Director. Together they work as program facilitators, educators, authors, and consultants specializing in holistic child development, education, and family dynamics. They co-created and developed Natural Learning Rhythms™(NLR)™, a holistic understanding of child development that honors wholeness and well-being in children. (NLR is the basis and philosophical foundation of many EnCompass programs; see the Bibliography.) Josette and Ba are the coauthors of four books: *Natural Learning Rhythms* (Celestial Arts, 1993); *Everyone Wins* (New Society Publishers, 1990); *Tiger by the Tail* (EnCompass Press, 1998); and the soon to be published *Rites of Passage: Stages of Life*. They have worked with thousands of families, teachers, and schools on all facets of relationship with children and have been using NLR for over 21 years.

Debra and Tom Weistar serve as the Outdoor Education Directors for EnCompass. Through outdoor education programs, the Weistars serve children, families, at-risk youth, schools, businesses, and individuals. They designed, built, and now facilitate the EnCompass Challenge Ropes Course, where many of the activities in this book were created and continue to be used on a regular basis. They have developed and used cooperative games, exercises, and initiatives to bring together people of all ages and backgrounds.

Amber and Albee Kara, program facilitators and educators, have been working with EnCompass for more than 10 years. Their experience covers a broad spectrum of traditional and nontraditional approaches to education and learning. In addition to being fully trained ropes course facilitators and outdoor educators, they co-lead outdoor adventure programs for children, seminars in child development, and Rites of Passage.

ABOUT ENCOMPASS

EnCompass, a nonprofit learning center located in California's Sierra Nevada foothills, offers a wide variety of seminars, programs, and services for the whole family. EnCompass is dedicated to supporting the well-being and wholeness of children and families through integrated holistic programs and facilities and through the development of Holistic Education in theory and practice. In carrying out that mission, we aspire to lead whole lives, contribute to that in others, honor relationships, and engage in lifelong learning.

EnCompass holds the simple contention that humans are born with inner capacities for well-being. By nurturing their inherent wholeness, individuals and families have the opportunity to actualize this well-being across the diversity of age, ethnicity, class, and culture. From parenting seminars and family programs to wilderness adventures and our many Holistic Education Initiatives, EnCompass strives to bring a holistic perspective and rigorous inquiry into a broad spectrum of learning opportunities.

EnCompass has recently completed its Conference Center, with lodging for 70, and its Education Center. Using a revolutionary method of super-adobe, as well as rammed earth technology, EnCompass hopes to serve as a model of durable structures and environmentally sensitive building techniques.

Please feel free to contact EnCompass for more information.

Mail: EnCompass
11011 Tyler Foote Road,
Nevada City, California 95959-9309
USA

Phone: 800-200-1107 or 530-292-1000
Fax: 530-292-1209

Email: connection@EnCompass-NLR.org
Website: www.EnCompass-NLR.org

More
Education & Parenting
titles available now from
New Society Publishers

EVERYONE WINS!

Cooperative Games and Activities

Josette & Ba Luvmour

E*veryone Wins!* is a handbook
of more than 150 cooperative
games and activities for enhanc-
ing conflict resolution and communication skills and building
self-esteem. All activities have
been tested and are graded
according to appropriate age
level (1+ to adult), size of group,
indoor or outdoor location, and
activity level, and include notes
on materials needed, special
hints and variations for group
leaders.

128 pages 5.5" x 8.5"

Games / Activities

US$8.95 / ISBN 0-86571-190- 9

Can$10.95 / ISBN 1-55092-011-1

CONNECTING KIDS
Exploring Diversity Together

Linda D. Hill

Foreword by Rick Scott

C hildren growing up today face differences of age, culture, language, heritage, lifestyle, religion, and physical ability at every turn. But without guidance, they tend to deal with differences by dividing up into in-groups and out-groups — resulting in exclusion, violence and bullying. *Connecting Kids* helps children explore and celebrate differences, building acceptance and an inclusive culture that prevents and reduces prejudice and discrimination. Focusing on 20 key skills, it includes over 200 fun games and activities that teach social, "connecting" behaviors. Well-illustrated, the book also includes "case study" stories and artwork from around the world for each skill, a complete cross-referenced index, and further resources.

Linda D. Hill is a psychologist, educator, writer, and child care worker who has focused for 30 years on diversity issues.

---

192 pages 8.5" x 11"

Over 100 B&W photographs & illustrations

Education & Teaching/Family & Parenting

ISBN 0-86571-431-2

US$19.95 / Can$25.95

A VOLCANO IN MY TUMMY

Helping Children to Handle Anger

Éliane Whitehouse and Warwick Pudney

A *Volcano in My Tummy* presents a clear and effective approach to helping children and adults alike understand and deal constructively with children's anger. The book offers engaging, well-organized activities which help to overcome the fear of children's anger which many adult caregivers experience, and distinguishes between anger the feeling, and violence the behavior. Primarily created for ages six to thirteen, it is accessible for use in class or at home.

80 pages 8.5" x 11"

40+ line drawings Exercises & Games

ISBN 0-86571-349-9

US$12.95 / Can $15.95

PLAYING WITH FIRE

Creative Conflict Resolution
for Young Adults

*Fiona Macbeth
and Nic Fine*

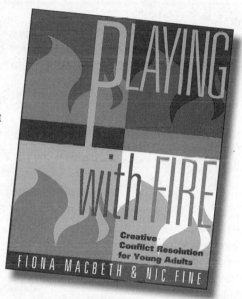

Playing with Fire extends the fast-growing field of conflict resolution to work with young adults. Drawing from successful programs in the US, Canada, and the UK, it presents a training program that helps young adults explore situations of conflict and interpersonal violence while learning and practicing skills and strategies for turning destructive conflicts into constructive dialogs. It is a practical, ready-to-use guide for teachers, counselors, group leaders, and others.

192 pages 8.5" x 11"

Exercises Handouts Reading list Index

US$19.95 / ISBN 0-86571-306-5

Can$24.95 / ISBN 1-55092-257-2

KEEPING THE PEACE
Practicing Cooperation and Conflict Resolution with Preschoolers

Susanne Wichert

Keeping the Peace is a handbook for parents, daycare providers, kindergarten teachers, and playgroup leaders striving to create harmonious groups, bolster children's self-esteem, and foster cooperative and creative interactions between kids aged from two and a half to six. It includes carefully designed and clearly presented activities, anecdotes from the author's own extensive journals, and the theories behind the design.

112 pages 8.5" x 11"

Exercises Photographs Bibliography

US$14.95 / ISBN 0-86571-158-5

Can$17.95 / ISBN 1-55092-031-6

TEACHING YOUNG CHILDREN IN VIOLENT TIMES

Building a Peaceable Classroom

Diane E. Levin

Teaching Young Children in Violent Times helps teachers and group leaders working with pre-K to 3rd-graders create an environment in which young children can learn alternatives to the violent behaviors modeled in our society, the media and home. It offers practical guidelines and activities for meeting young children's needs for safety; helping them learn to appreciate diversity; and providing opportunities and skills to resolve conflicts creatively and respectfully.

176 pages 8.5" x 11"

Illustrations Dialogs Bibliography Index

Educators for Social Responsibility

US$21.95 / ISBN 0-86571-316-2

Can$24.95 / ISBN 1-55092-261-0

DUMBING US DOWN

The Hidden Curriculum of Compulsory Schooling

John Gatto

Foreword by
Thomas Moore

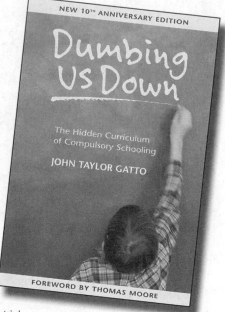

With over 70,000 copies of the first edition in print, this radical treatise on public education has been a New Society Publishers' bestseller for 10 years! Thirty years of award-winning teaching in New York City's public schools led John Gatto to the sad conclusion that compulsory governmental schooling does little but teach young people to follow orders like cogs in an industrial machine. This second edition includes a new foreword by Thomas Moore, a new afterword from the author, and a new introduction.

John Gatto has been a teacher for 30 years and is a recipient of the New York State Teacher of the Year award.

---

144 pages 6" x 9"

Education & Teaching / Current Affairs

ISBN 0-86571-448-7

US$11.95 / Can$14.95 — available February 2002

THE NATURAL CHILD
Parenting from the Heart

Jan Hunt

Foreword by Peggy O'Mara,
Mothering Magazine

The *Natural Child* makes a
compelling case for a return
to attachment parenting, a child-
rearing approach that has come
naturally for parents throughout
most of human history. In this
insightful guide, parenting spe-
cialist Jan Hunt links together
attachment parenting principles with child advocacy and
homeschooling philosophies,
offering a consistent
approach to raising a loving,
trusting, and confident child.
The Natural Child explains
the value of extended
breast-feeding, family co-sleeping, and
minimal child-parent separation. It also guides the reader through home-
school approaches that support attachment parenting principles.

"...magnificent; truly, simply, to the point; written with admirable clarity
and economy; and of enormous importance. I can't praise it sufficiently." —
Joseph Chilton Pearce, author of *The Magical Child*

Jan Hunt, from Oregon, is a parenting counselor and Director of The
Natural Child Project. She is a contributor to *Mothering, Empathic Parenting*,
and *Growing Without Schooling*.

192 pages 6" x 9"

Family & Parenting / Education & Teaching / Relationships

ISBN 0-86571-440-1

US$14.95 / Can$18.95

If you have enjoyed *Win-Win Games for All Ages*, you might also enjoy other

BOOKS TO BUILD A NEW SOCIETY

Our books provide positive solutions for people who
want to make a difference. We specialize in:

Sustainable Living • Ecological Design and Planning

Natural Building & Appropriate Technology • New Forestry

Environment and Justice • Conscientious Commerce

Progressive Leadership • Resistance and Community • Nonviolence

Educational and Parenting Resources

For a full list of NSP's titles, please call **1-800-567-6772** *or check out our web site at:*

www.newsociety.com

New Society Publishers

ENVIRONMENTAL BENEFITS STATEMENT

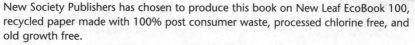

New Society Publishers has chosen to produce this book on New Leaf EcoBook 100,
recycled paper made with 100% post consumer waste, processed chlorine free, and
old growth free.

For every 5,000 books printed, New Society saves the following resources:[1]

28	Trees
2,527	Pounds of Solid Waste
2,781	Gallons of Water
3,627	Kilowatt Hours of Electricity
4,594	Pounds of Greenhouse Gases
20	Pounds of HAPs, VOCs, and AOX Combined
7	Cubic Yards of Landfill Space

---

[1]Environmental benefits are calculated based on research done by the Environmental Defense Fund and
other members of the Paper Task Force who study the environmental impacts of the paper industry.

For more information on this environmental benefits statement, or to inquire about environmentally
friendly papers, please contact New Leaf Paper – info@newleafpaper.com Tel: 888 • 989 • 5323.

NEW SOCIETY PUBLISHERS